LOVE THE LEAST (A LOT)

MICHAEL SPIELMAN

LOXAFAMOSITY

Love the Least (A Lot)

Copyright © 2013 by Michael Spielman

Published by Loxafamosity Ministries, Inc.
            PO Box 9291
            Moscow, ID 83843

First Printing, 2013

ISBN: 978-0-615-79271-2

to Carrie:

Thank you for marrying into this madness.

Thank you for staying. I love you.

Author's Note:

The bulk of this book was written in 2011; much of 2012 was spent in search of a publisher. Time and again, I ran into variations of the same two responses: *Books on abortion don't sell. Christians already know that abortion is wrong.* The first sentiment is undoubtedly true. I have my doubts about the second—which is why I released *LOVE THE LEAST*, sans publisher, as a free ebook on the 40-year anniversary of *Roe vs. Wade*. I've since realized that there are still large numbers of people who can't or won't read ebooks—which is where this version comes in. Though I can't afford to give the print copies away for free, I pray they will help further expand the reach of this vital message.

Contents

LOVE THE LEAST (A LOT)

FOR THE PAST 12 YEARS, the whole of my vocational life has been devoted to combating abortion. I suppose it's natural for this book to follow suit, but abortion is only part of the equation. I have something bigger in view—and I don't say that lightly. Abortion is easily the most significant social justice issue of our era; it could hardly be more important. But in the context of eternity, abortion is a blip on the radar.

Don't get me wrong. It is crucial to get the abortion question right. Millions of lives hang in the balance. But it is imperative to get the Jesus question right. Eternity hangs in the balance. If I'm right about abortion but wrong about Jesus, I miss everything. It's like knowing all the answers for a test, but showing up at the wrong classroom. It may seem a small detail, but it trumps all the rest. Of all the questions in life, the Jesus question is the only one we can't afford to miss.

Saying that, you may wonder why I bother with abortion at all. Why not preach Christ and let everything else work itself out? Truth be told, that is exactly what I did throughout my high school and college careers. I focused on the problem (man's separation from God), and rationalized that the symptoms (like abortion) would eventually take care of themselves. I was wrong. And not just from a practical standpoint. I was wrong from a gospel standpoint.

The reason we can't leave the public condemnation of abortion by the wayside is precisely *because* of the eternal centrality of Jesus Christ. In much of the world today, you're not being a faithful witness for Christ if you're not being a faithful witness *against* abortion. I don't know how else to say it. If your response to abortion is wrong, your response to Jesus is wrong. If you've distanced yourself from the open condemnation of abortion, you've distanced yourself from Christ.

I'll spend the better part of this book trying to biblically demonstrate why I feel justified in making such an explicit connection between devotion to Christ and opposition to abortion. For now I'll simply point you in that direction by explaining the title. *LOVE THE LEAST* references the story of the sheep and the goats found in Matthew 25. In this judgment account, Jesus identifies himself with the helpless and oppressed, warning that whatever we fail to do for them, we fail to do for him. Those who have performed tangible acts of love for the "least of these" are ushered into eternity with Christ. Those who failed to love the least are ushered into eternal torment.

You would be hard-pressed to find a group of people more qualified to wear the "least of these" label than abortion-vulnerable children. They are the most helpless members of the human community. Around the globe, more than

100,000 are killed each day—and hardly anyone notices. Some argue (as I once did) that devotion to Christ precludes focused involvement on the abortion front. Biblically speaking, that is a gross misunderstanding. It is devotion to Christ that should prompt our involvement on the abortion front. Abortion would be a far less important issue were it not for the centrality of Jesus Christ. We wouldn't have to give it nearly so much thought if Jesus hadn't inserted himself into the equation by judging our love for him on our love for the least.

At this point, let me reassure you that my intention is not to take the gloriously broad "least of these" banner and reduce it to a single, narrow application. I have no desire to downplay the myriad other global injustices that call for focused, Christ-exalting engagement on behalf of the "least" among us. But neither do I want to be guilty of holding my tongue where it cost me the most. God's people can and should be a voice against poverty, disease, child soldiering, sex trafficking, forced prostitution, and all the rest. But there is a huge, eternal danger in leaving abortion off that list—and not just as it applies to the fate of unborn children. If we are only willing to take on causes championed by the rest of the world, if we're only willing to raise our voice in support of those issues celebrated by the popular culture around us, it's fair to ask whether our devotion is to Christ at all.

In writing this book, I have three audiences in mind. The first is comprised of those who are already combating the injustice of abortion. My prayer for you is that you would reexamine your devotion to this cause in light of eternity.

Are you doing this through the grace of God, for the love of your Savior, in the joy of the Spirit? Or has it simply become a battle to win or a notch to register in your belt of holiness? Are you doing this to earn God's favor or because you have God's favor?

The second audience is comprised of those who love Christ, but have largely avoided the public condemnation of abortion. My prayer for you is that you would come to recognize that the neglect of abortion-vulnerable children is nothing less than the neglect of Jesus Christ. I don't say this to be gimmicky or cute, but in the simple conviction that you can't love Jesus as he's called you to if you're failing to expose the evil of abortion.

The third audience is comprised of those who claim no special allegiance to Jesus and see nothing intrinsically wrong with abortion. If that's you, what a remarkable thing that this book is in your hands. Don't give up on me yet. Don't think there's nothing here for you. I've had you in mind from the beginning. Plenty of people have had their eyes opened to the glory of Christ through the context of abortion. I pray you'll join their ranks. Right now, you might see devotion to Christ and opposition to abortion as small, bitter, angry, self-righteous things. They are not. If they've been expressed that way to you, I apologize. It was a mischaracterization. And if it's issues like abortion that are keeping you out of church in the first place, read on. As you'll see through the course of this book, abortion is a microcosm of life's most fundamental problem. The solution to one is the solution to both.

On the surface *LOVE THE LEAST* is a book about abortion. At its heart this is a book about the love of Jesus Christ. And whether you recognize it yet or not, that is something none of us can live without.

Chapter One

A BIBLICAL VIEW OF UNBORN LIFE

AS A FRESHMAN IN COLLEGE, I had one explanation for why abortion is wrong: Revelation 1:18. *God holds the keys to life and death—not men.* That was good enough for me, but it didn't go very far in public debate. I remember sitting in my dorm room one day, listening to my roommate try to convince the girls who lived above us that abortion is immoral. I quickly convinced myself that it was a hopeless endeavor. Since they didn't believe the Bible, I didn't even open my mouth.

Because I had framed the abortion issue in such narrow, spiritual terms, I had almost no capacity to demonstrate its injustice. And so I stayed quiet. All these years later, it's ironic that I so often condemn abortion on scientific grounds while my opponents defend it on pseudo-religious grounds. I argue that abortion kills a living human being; they argue that they're not yet persons. I argue that there is no debate regarding the biological beginning of human life; they argue that there is more to being human than biology. I argue that embryos and fetuses are just as human as we are; they argue that they don't have a soul (even if they call it something else).

Though it's commonly assumed that the arguments against abortion are spiritually rooted while those for it are secularly rooted, it is often the reverse. All of the more sophisticated "pro-choice" claims are spiritual in nature, and it can actually be easier to argue against abortion from biology than from the Bible. After all, the word "abortion" never appears in Scripture. But that doesn't mean the Bible is silent about abortion. Appealing to God's Word may not influence the fuzzy spirituality of the unbelieving abortion advocate, but I want to emphasize from the start that the Bible offers clear and compelling arguments against abortion. The outright promotion of abortion, and the softer tolerance of abortion are both incompatible with a biblical worldview.

For all of us who were not born ahead of schedule, our time in the womb was a nine-month period of life—just as kindergarten was a nine-month period of life. Scripture doesn't provide a specific prohibition against killing kindergartners. We know it's wrong because it falls under the much broader banner of the sixth commandment: *you shall not murder*. More specifically, we know it's wrong because it is incompatible with the character of God. When Pharaoh commanded the Hebrew midwives to execute all of the newborn males,[1] they did not have a specific prohibition against infanticide to guide them. They didn't even have the Ten Commandments, but they feared God, and that

---

1   Exodus 1:15-16

was enough. When Cain killed Abel,[2] he was not violating a written prohibition, but in knowing God, he knew what God required. Cain makes no attempt to claim ignorance when God curses him for murdering his brother. Even in the absence of a specific prohibition, the commandments can be inferred from the character of God. They are the natural expression of who God is.

Scripture is sufficient to make us "competent [and] equipped for every good work."[3] It doesn't specifically address every dilemma that befalls us, but it gives us the necessary framework to work through them. The Bible speaks to abortion as it speaks to every topic under the sun—by teaching us who God is and what he requires of us. If the Hebrew midwives had enjoyed the benefit of a completed cannon, they still wouldn't have found an explicit prohibition against infanticide—anymore than we find a specific prohibition against abortion. The reason it's wrong to kill a child in the classroom or a child in the womb is because it's wrong to murder. Age doesn't change anything. And the reason it's wrong to murder is not because it was written on a stone tablet thousands of years ago. It's wrong because it assaults the character and authority of God.

Almost nobody[4] argues that it is inappropriate to apply the prohibition against murder to infants or school children.

---

2   Genesis 4:8

3   II Timothy 3:17

4   Prominent author and philosopher, Peter Singer, is one of the few abortion advocates who also advocates for infanticide. For further study, see: "Abortion Ethics in a Christ-Haunted Culture" (http://www.abort73.com/ blog/abortion_ethics_in_a_christ-haunted_culture/)

Lots of people argue the inappropriateness of applying it to children in the womb—and take great issue with even calling them "children." Over the years I've dialogued with plenty of angry abortion advocates—mostly on college campuses. To them, referring to an unborn human being as a "baby" is a scandalous assertion. How many times have I heard this retort: *"It's not a baby, it's a fetus!"*? In the modern vernacular, "fetus" (which is Latin for "offspring") has become a term of derision, strategically wielded by those seeking to dehumanize babies in the womb. In reality, it's just a marker of development—like "infant" or "toddler" (imagine hearing a new parent yell, *"It's not a baby, it's an infant!"*). Baby is a broad word. Fetus is a narrow word. Both are correct. Nevertheless, you can tell a lot about someone's position on abortion by noting which of these words one uses. Since this chapter begins our examination of what *God* thinks about abortion, let's take a look at what kinds of words he uses—through the authors of Scripture.[5]

Though the Bible does not directly mention abortion, it makes frequent reference to pregnancy and birth. The question we need to answer is this: Does the Bible give any indication that human beings inside the womb should be regarded as categorically *different* from human beings outside the womb? Our first scriptural glimpse at life in the womb comes in Genesis 25:22. Isaac's wife, Rebekah, is pregnant with twins. The verse tells us that, "the children struggled

---

5   By way of disclaimer, I'm a layman. I've never been to seminary; I can't read Hebrew or Greek. But I've read the Bible many times through over the years and have qualified friends and resources at my disposal. What I lack in formal training, I try to make up for in earnest study and devotion.

together within her." The Hebrew word can be translated as "children" or "sons." It is first used in Genesis 3:16 when God decrees the penalty for Adam and Eve's rebellion: "I will surely multiply your pain in child bearing (literally, "children you shall bore with•pain"[6])." The same word is used in Genesis 10:21 to describe the children of Shem and in Genesis 11:5 to indicate who built the tower of Babel (the "children of man"). It is used five more times before the account of Rebekah in reference to children who are already born.[7]

In the New Testament, we see the same thing. The word "baby" (brephos) is used interchangeably to describe babies inside and outside the womb. In Luke 1:41, Elizabeth is pregnant with John the Baptist. Luke, who was a physician by trade, refers to John as "the baby in her womb." In the next chapter, the same word is used to describe Jesus: "you will find a baby wrapped in swaddling cloths."[8] The first indication that God does not view children in the womb as categorically different from those outside the womb is the fact that he calls them the same thing. He calls them children; he calls them babies. For most of human history, the rest of the world has followed suit. The only people who take issue with applying the word "baby" to an unborn human being are those seeking to justify abortion. Planned Parenthood, after all, doesn't schedule appointments to abort your baby. They schedule appointments to terminate your pregnancy. For all the times Scripture speaks of life in the womb, an equivalent for the

---

6   C. van der Merwe, *Lexham Hebrew-English Interlinear Bible*; Bible. O.T. Hebrew (Logos Research Systems, Inc., 2004).

7   Genesis 17:17, 18:19, 21:7, 22:20, 25:4

8   Luke 2:12

word "fetus" is never used,[9] and that is of no small significance. Anyone who has an interest in justifying abortion does not talk the way the Bible talks.

Our second point of examination lies not in the words God uses to describe unborn children, but in the things he ascribes to them. Returning to the account of Jacob and Esau in the womb, did you notice what these twin boys were doing before they were even born? They were struggling. Literally, they "jostled"[10] each other. In recounting a brief, personal

---

9   It should be noted that in Numbers 5:28, the literal word "seed" has been rendered "children" in many English translations. In the ESV, the text reads, "she shall be free and shall conceive children." The literal, Hebrew rendering is, "she-is-innocent and•she-is-sown seed." Some may point to this and suggest that it is an example of God using sub-human language to describe human offspring early in pregnancy. There are a number of reasons why the use of "seed" in this context is not comparable to the dehumanizing use of "fetus" in the modern vernacular. Seed is a broad word in Hebrew as it is in English. It is much less specific than fetus. At various points in Scripture, it is translated as "children," "offspring," "conceiving" (literally, seeding), "semen," and of course, "seed." Four times in Leviticus, the word "seed" refers to born children—as it does in 1 Samuel 2:20. The word "seed" is translated as "offspring" close to 200 times in the Old Testament. More than 40 of those instances reference living descendants, making it impossible to argue that "seed" refers to potential human beings instead of actual human beings. On a number of occasions, "seed" references specific people—making it impossible to argue that its use implies a lack of individual personhood. In fact, Scripture's first reference to the coming of Christ is couched in the word "seed" (Genesis 3:15). *There will be enmity between the seed of the woman and the seed of the serpant, but the seed of the woman will crush the head of the seed of the serpant.* The word "seed" is frequently used to reference the promised line of Abraham, Isaac, and Jacob, and in the New Testament, Jesus is described as the seed of David in John 7:42, Acts 13:23, Romans 1:3, and 2 Timothy 2:8. In Galatians 3:16, Jesus is called the seed of Abraham. Paul calls himself a seed of Abraham in Romans 11:1. All that to say, the use of the word "seed" in Numbers 5:28 is not an example of God applying a sub-human term to children in the womb.

10 C. van der Merwe, *Lexham Hebrew-English Interlinear Bible*; Bible. O.T. Hebrew. (Logos Research Systems, Inc., 2004).

history of Jacob, the prophet Hosea says, "in the womb he took his brother by the heel, and in manhood he strove with God."[11] One event happened before birth. The other event happened long after birth. Both are stories from Jacob's past, and they are recounted side by side.

More remarkable still is the account Luke gives us of John the Baptist. We read in Luke 1:15 that John was filled with the Holy Spirit *in the womb*. When John's mother, Elizabeth, visits her cousin, the mother of the Christ, John "leaped" at the sound of Mary's voice. In Luke 1:44, Elizabeth proclaims that, "when the sound of [Mary's] greeting came to my ears, the baby in my womb leaped for joy." And lest you discredit this attribution of joy as the mere fancy of a giddy mom, verse 41 tells us that Elizabeth was filled with the Holy Spirit when she said it. John the Baptist was filled with the Spirit in the womb, and he leaped for joy at his first encounter with Jesus—who was still in the womb himself. Why is this significant? Because in the created order, it is only *people* who are filled with the Holy Spirit.

In Judges 13:5, an angel of the Lord prophesies about the conception and birth of Samson with the following announcement: "for behold, you shall conceive and bear a son. No razor shall come upon his head, for the child shall be a Nazirite to God *from the womb*, and he shall begin to save Israel from the hand of the Philistines" (emphasis added). The word used to describe this child, this Nazirite in the womb, is the same word used in Genesis 25:22, and the same word that is used throughout the Old Testament to describe

---

11 Hosea 12:3

born children. More to the point, notice the charge the angel gives to Samson's mother in the verse preceding: "Therefore be careful and drink no wine or strong drink, and eat nothing unclean." Why? Because this child shall be a Nazarite to God *from the womb*. Nazirites are not to consume strong drink after birth, and they are not to consume strong drink before birth.

When Samson is grown and foolishly reveals the secret of his strength to Delilah, he traces his Nazirite history all the way back to the womb: "I have been a Nazirite to God from my mother's womb."[12] Notice that Samson uses the personal pronoun, "I" to describe himself in the womb. *I was a Nazirite of God in the womb.* And Samson is not alone in speaking of his time in the womb in very personal terms. In Job 10:18-19, we find Job in the depths of despair, so consumed with grief that he laments his very existence. He asks God, "Why did you bring me out from the womb? Would that I had died before any eye had seen me and were as though I had not been, carried from the womb to the grave." Though the literal rendering of these verses is hard to decipher, I am struck by two things. First, Job recognizes that he really existed in his mother's womb. Second, to have died in the womb, he says, would have been "as though" he had never been, but not quite. He sees life and death in the womb as real things—as personal things. His remarks run parallel to those found in Jeremiah 20:16-18. Battling significant despair of his own, Jeremiah wonders why the Lord, "did not kill me in the womb; so my mother would have been my grave… Why

---

12 Judges 16:17

did I come out from the womb to see toil and sorrow, and spend my days in shame?" These are bleak ponderings, but notice what they indicate. These heroes of old did not view their lives in the womb as times of pre-existence. They saw themselves as being really alive with the capacity to really die.

In the first chapter of Jeremiah, the prophet recounts his calling this way: "Now the word of the Lord came to me, saying, 'Before I formed you in the womb I knew you, and before you were born I consecrated you; I appointed you a prophet to the nations.'"[13] Jeremiah was set apart as a sacred, holy vessel unto the Lord, a prophet to the nations—not after he was born but before. In fact, God knew Jeremiah before he was even conceived. Try arguing that point to the secular skeptic! In God's economy, we are not only persons before birth, we are persons before conception. On some level, God knows us before we exist. The prophet Isaiah says that God called him and named him in the womb.[14] In Psalm 22:10, King David declares that, "from my mother's womb you have been my God." And if we jump back to the verse preceding, we get a better sense of what he means by that. "You are he who took me from the womb; you made me trust you at my mother's breasts." God's protection of David in the womb and his provision for David as a nursing babe were the earliest indicators that God could be trusted—that God would provide. Psalm 71:6 reads, "Upon you I have leaned from before my birth; you are he who took me from my mother's womb." The authors of Scripture do not speak as

---

13 Jeremiah 1:5
14 Isaiah 49:1

if our personal histories begin at birth. They speak as if they begin much earlier.

Perhaps the best known "pro-life" passage is Psalm 139. It opens with David's marveling at the depth and intimacy of God's knowledge of him. God sees all; God knows all. There is no place we can escape from his presence. David suggests that the foundation of God's intimate knowledge of us is the fact that he made us: "For you formed my inward parts; you knitted me together in my mother's womb. I praise you, for I am fearfully and wonderfully made… my frame was not hidden from you, when I was being made in secret, intricately woven in the depths of the earth. Your eyes saw my unformed substance; in your book were written, every one of them, the days that were formed for me, when as yet there were none of them."[15]

In Isaiah 49:5, God traces his authority and calling over Isaiah back to the fact that he "formed [Isaiah] from the womb to be his servant." A few chapters earlier, Isaiah prefaces his address to the nation Israel with the reminder that the Lord "formed you from the womb and will help you."[16] God can be trusted because he formed you in the womb; he took care of you when you were most vulnerable.

When Job maintains his innocence before his accusing friends, he ties his consistent kindness towards his servants to the fact that God made them both in the womb. Job goes on to point out that he has never withheld from the poor. He has never turned the widow or fatherless away hungry. He has

---

15 Psalm 139:13-16
16 Isaiah 44:2

become as a father to them, clothing the needy so that none could complain of his generosity. Why? Job answers with two questions: "Did not he who made me in the womb make him? And did not one fashion us in the womb?"[17] God is the active force driving our development in the womb. That fact brought praise to the mouth of David, brought purpose and comfort to Isaiah, and compelled Job to treat all as equals. For us, it should do that and more. If God is performing a "wonderful work" in the womb," if he "knitted" each of us together in secret, if God's provision and protection in the womb is to be the foundation for our lifelong trust in him, can there really be any question as to God's view of abortion—which forcefully invades the womb to intentionally destroy the person God is creating?

Because of the words God uses to describe children in the womb, because of the types of things God ascribes to children in the womb, because so many of the Bible's personal histories are tied to the womb, and because God is regularly identified as the one at work in the womb, I cannot help but conclude that God expects us to treat children inside the womb with as much dignity, care, and respect as we would treat children outside the womb. There is simply no indication in Scripture that the lives of unborn children should be viewed as insignificant or expendable. Having said that, I can anticipate at least one potential objection. When John the Baptist leaped for joy in his mother's womb, Elizabeth was at least six months into her pregnancy.[18] If we assume that all of

---

17 Job 31:15
18 Luke 1:36

Scripture's references to children in the womb refer to babies nearer birth than conception, how can we be certain what God's view of unborn children is during the first trimester of pregnancy, when close to 90% of all abortions occur?[19]

At the crux of this objection is the idea that aborting early in pregnancy is morally superior to aborting late in pregnancy. Though I don't think most Christians make this distinction, it is extremely prevalent in the world at large. Statistically speaking, 66% of the Americans surveyed in a 2003 Gallup poll believe abortion should be legal during the first trimester; only 10% believe abortion should be legal during the third trimester.[20] One of the best ways to demonstrate the fallacy of making such distinctions is to examine the basic biology of prenatal development, which we'll do in chapter three. From conception on, human development is a continuum. The only differences between children early in pregnancy and children late in pregnancy are the differences that don't matter. More to the context at hand, there are a number of ways to respond to this objection from the pages of Scripture.

Of the texts we've looked at so far, many of them have just as much application to early pregnancy as they do to late pregnancy. When the angel commands Samson's mother to not drink any wine for the sake of the Nazirite in her womb,

---

19 "Facts on Induced Abortion in the United States." Guttmacher Institute, August 2011. <http://www.guttmacher.org/pubs/fb_induced_abortion.html>.

20 Saad, Lydia. "Americans Agree With Banning 'Partial-Birth Abortion.'" Gallup, Inc, 6 Nov. 2003. <http://www.gallup.com/poll/9658/Americans-Agree-Banning-PartialBirth-Abortion.aspx>.

it is not a prohibition that applies only to the second or third trimesters. It is given before conception. When David traces his personal history back to the womb, he takes it all the way back to conception: "in sin did my mother conceive me."[21] The bride of Solomon does the same thing when she references, "the chamber of her who conceived me."[22] And without question, all of the references to being formed in the womb are especially applicable to the first trimester, since virtually all of the "forming" takes place during the first eight weeks. It has also struck me that starting in Genesis 4:1 and progressing throughout the Old Testament, there is a consistent pairing of conception and birth in Scripture's family narratives: "Now Adam knew Eve his wife, and she conceived and bore Cain... Cain knew his wife, and she conceived and bore Enoch... Sarah conceived and bore Abraham a son... Leah conceived and bore a son."[23] The list goes on and on and on. "Bilhah conceived and bore Jacob a son."[24] Wouldn't it have been more efficient to simply say, "Bilhah bore Jacob a son"? Though we can't say for certain why the biblical authors were so often compelled to preface birth accounts with conception (literally "becoming pregnant") accounts, it is not unreasonable to conclude that God is giving special significance to both the sexual act of becoming pregnant and the decisive beginning of a new human life.

Depending on the translation you're using, there are only 1-3 times that the word "conception" appears

---

21 Psalm 51:5
22 Song of Solomon 3:4
23 Genesis 4:1, 4:17, 21:2, 29:32
24 Genesis 30:5

in the English Bible. Hosea 9:11 is the verse that is most consistently translated to include the word "conception." It reads: "As for Ephraim, their glory shall fly away like a bird—No birth, no pregnancy, and no conception! (literally, "conception of biological life"[25]). This same word has been translated "conception" in Ruth 4:13: "So Boaz took Ruth and she became his wife; and when he went in to her, the Lord gave her conception (literally "conception to·her Yahweh and·(he) gave to·her"[26]), and she bore a son." There are two things to note. First, God is not only the one who forms children in the womb once the process has started, he is the one who divinely decrees that the process start in the first place. *God gave her conception.* Second, in declaring a curse upon Ephraim, Hosea starts with the blessing of birth and works backwards to conception. Notice that he doesn't say, *no conception, no implantation, no heartbeat, no brain wave activity, no viability outside the womb,* etc. The only decisive moments are conception and birth—indicating again that there is no biblical line of demarcation in the womb, where we go from being a non-child to a child.

Finally, I'd like to point you to Ecclesiastes 11:5: "As you do not know the way the spirit comes to the bones in the womb of a woman with child, so you do not know the work of God who makes everything." We are ignorant of when and how God imparts a human soul to a developing body. We are also ignorant of how and when God removes that human soul

---

25 C. van der Merwe, *Lexham Hebrew-English Interlinear Bible*; Bible. O.T. Hebrew (Logos Research Systems, Inc., 2004).

26 C. van der Merwe.

from the body at the point of death. What we do know is that God merges spirit and body somewhere in the womb. Our inability to pinpoint the exact point at which this happens should not lead us to conclude that abortion is permissible. It should compel the very opposite. If there is uncertainty as to when the spirit of a human being enters the body of a human being, we must error on the side of protecting life, not on the side of destroying it.

I will draw this chapter to a close by quickly examining two specific texts that have been used (mostly by those outside the church) to argue that God does *not* condemn abortion. The first text is Exodus 21:22-25:

> When men strive together and hit a pregnant woman, so that her children come out, but there is no harm, the one who hit her shall surely be fined, as the woman's husband shall impose on him, and he shall pay as the judges determine. But if there is harm, then you shall pay life for life, eye for eye, tooth for tooth, hand for hand, foot for foot, burn for burn, wound for wound, stripe for stripe.

On the surface, it may be hard to imagine how this text could possibly be used in the defense of abortion. It seems an almost conclusive prohibition *against* abortion. A pregnant woman is struck and she goes into labor prematurely. If no harm comes as a result of the early delivery, the accidental assailant is fined. If harm does result from the premature birth, the guilty man shall pay: wound for wound, life for life. This, however, is not the way everyone interprets the passage. Some believe that what is being spoken of is a miscarriage. If no harm comes *to the mother* as a result of the assault and miscarriage, a fine shall be issued. If harm does come to the mother, the punishment will be in accordance to her injuries. On this interpretation, abortion-advocates argue that since a monetary fine is all that is required for the miscarriage, the death of a child in the womb must be a relatively insignificant thing.

For the sake of argument, let's assume that the miscarriage interpretation is the correct one. Does that mean we can use this passage as a biblical justification for abortion? Pastor Jack Hughes notes that there are four reasons why we cannot.[27] First, this passage refers to an accidental injury. Abortion is intentionally fatal. Second, the fact that a penalty is required at all indicates that it was wrong for the baby to die. Third, the law of Moses does not generally require the death penalty for accidental death. Fourth, the fact that a lesser penalty is afforded to the child than to the mother in no way indicates that the child is less of a human person than the mother. In the preceding verses, a lesser penalty is required of the master who accidentally kills his slave, who is without question a human person.

Having said all that, there is strong evidence that the miscarriage interpretation is not the correct one. The word

_____

27 Hughes, Jack. "Biblical Principles for Key Social Issues: Abortion." Calvary Bible Church, n.d. <http://www.calvarybiblechurch.org/home/180007650/180007745/180059418/7%20Abortion.pdf>.

Moses uses in verse 22 for "children come out" is the same word he used in Genesis 25:26 to describe a normal, live birth. Elsewhere in Scripture, Moses does use the normal Hebrew word for miscarriage, as he does two chapters later in Exodus 23:26. Furthermore, the word Moses uses for "harm" does not indicate the child or the mother. It is left indefinite. If it was meant to apply exclusively to the mother, a feminine pronoun would have accompanied it. Moses uses the normal Hebrew word for "children" and the normal Hebrew word for "birth." There is no reason to think this refers to a miscarriage. And to borrow Pastor Hughes' conclusion: "The fact that this is the only place in all of the Bible where the death penalty is required for accidental death is significant. It shows us the value God places on both mothers and their unborn children. The death of either the mother or her child by accident would bring with it the death penalty!"[28]

The second passage in question is Numbers 5:27, and it's a head-scratcher. In Numbers 5:11-28, Moses lays out an elaborate ritual for uncovering the secret sin of adultery. If a wife is suspected of adultery, she is brought before the priest, where holy water is mixed with dust from the tabernacle floor (vs 16) and ink from the priest's written curse (vs 23). The woman must then swear an oath that if she has lain with another man, her body will be cursed upon drinking the water of bitterness. What is the bodily curse? In the ESV we read:

> And when he has made her drink the water,
> then, if she has defiled herself and has broken

---

28 Hughes, Jack.

> faith with her husband, the water that brings
> the curse shall enter into her and cause bitter
> pain, and her womb shall swell, and her thigh
> shall fall away, and the woman shall become
> a curse among her people.

The phrase, "her thigh shall fall away," is an extremely perplexing one. One literal translation renders it this way: the "belly-of•her" is "turgid," the "thigh–of•her...falls(-away)."[29] Commentators have been wrestling with this one for a long time. The translators of the NIV have rendered "her thigh shall fall away" as "her womb will miscarry." This wording has led some to argue that Numbers 5 references nothing less than a priestly formula for abortion. For my part, I will simply note that here again, the normal word for miscarriage is not used. We don't know what it means exactly for a thigh to fall away. The reason some tie it to pregnancy is because of the declaration in verse 28, that if the woman is innocent, she will be free of all guilt and able to have children. Clearly, one of the curses being prescribed to the adulterous woman is barrenness. Whether or not that includes the miscarriage of a child conceived through adultery is less certain.

What we can be sure of is that this passage in no way justifies abortion. If a miscarriage has taken place, it is because God decreed it, not because the priest gave her an abortifacient. Dirty water does not end a pregnancy. The curse was not in the water itself, but in the judgment of God.

---

29 *Hebrew Interlinear Bible (OT).* (Scripture4all Foundation, 2008). <http:// www.scripture4all.org>.

If God decrees that the penalty of adultery will be the loss of the child, that is his prerogative and well within his authority. He did as much through the death of David and Bathsheba's first child. Returning to the text I opened with, God holds the keys of Death and Hades. As Creator God, he had the authority to tell Abraham to sacrifice his son, Isaac. We do not share that same authority—even when the circumstances of conception are suspect. The lineage of Christ was marred by nothing less than fornicators, adulterers, prostitutes, and rapists.[30] While that doesn't make such behavior any less wicked, it certainly indicates that children conceived out of sexual immorality are no less valuable. God is at work in every conception—even those that begin as a result of sin.

Having now come to the end of our initial survey of Scripture, one driven by the desire to know God's opinion of abortion, I must confess that part of me feels this has been an exercise in the absurd. I have taken a number of pages to dive into the minutia of ancient words to prove something that should be abundantly obvious. God is not pro-abortion. The compassionate and merciful Creator of the universe opposes the violent destruction of the most innocent and helpless members of his most prized creation. Perhaps the chief reason that abortion isn't explicitly addressed in the Bible is because its wickedness should be so abundantly apparent to all. Leon

---

30 Though Scripture does not explicitly indict King David of rape, I still believe his behavior warrants the label. At the very least, what he did to Bathsheba is comparable to statutory rape: the blatant abuse of power, influence, and authority to take sexual advantage of a subject under his rule. See Richard M. Davidson's case study, "Did King David Rape Bathsheba?" for further explanation: http://www.atsjats.org/publication_file.php?pub_id=318&journal=1&type=pdf

Kass calls it the "wisdom of repugnance"—the idea that "some of the deepest moral matters that human beings have to deal with are not conveyed by rational arguments of the sort that professors of philosophy enjoy raising with their students and their colleagues."[31] He notes that "rational arguments can't really explain the taboos against incest or eating human flesh, or even why murder and adultery are abominations," but that we react against these things viscerally. He calls it "a good thing" that we don't have to "depend upon some moral philosopher's perfectly persuasive argument to keep us from staying our hand in all of these [atrocities]."[32]

The first time that my own young children were exposed to pictures of abortion, they knew intrinsically that something was dreadfully wrong. They needed no extra convincing—no biblical exegesis to demonstrate that abortion is not something God smiles on. But for all of us who are better schooled in rationalizing deplorable behavior, I offer this chapter as further "proof" that abortion is immoral and unjust. To say that the Bible is silent about abortion is like saying the Bible is silent about evangelism (another word that doesn't appear in the pages of Scripture). Even should the wisdom of repugnance not exist, the Bible gives us plenty of reasons to attribute to God the unequivocal opposition to abortion. In the pages that follow, those reasons will multiply.

---

31 Kass, Leon. "Interview with Leon Kass." AlbertMohler.com. R. Albert Mohler, Jr, 29 Nov. 2010. <http://www.albertmohler.com/2010/12/01/seeking-wisdom-for-a-modern-world-a-conversation-with-leon-kass-2/>.

32 Kass, Leon.

Chapter Two

A BIBLICAL VIEW OF CHILD SACRIFICE

BECAUSE OF THE WORK I DO, my children have grown up in the shadow of abortion. For better or worse, they have been exposed to it from their infancy. Last year, my wife, Carrie, told me of an exchange in our daughter Melanie's first grade class. As the students took turns telling the class what their mom or dad does for a living, Melanie seemed a little perplexed when her turn arrived. The public-school teacher, who has some familiarity with Abort73, asked her if I was an author? Melanie said no. The teacher then asked if I was an artist? No again. "My daddy tries to save babies from abortion," Melanie finally said. She later told Carrie that she wanted to be careful what she said because she didn't want to scare the other kids: "They would freak out if I told them what abortion was."

I have often encountered Christian parents who have deep concerns about exposing their children to the existence of abortion. I sympathize with those concerns but am regularly amazed by the sensitivity and insight children often display. After a year or more of pleading, it was my son, Seth, who finally convinced me to make Abort73 shirts for kids. Whether my rationale was legitimate or not, I didn't want to give the impression that we were using children to promote a message. I've seen "pro-choice" parents dress their babies in shirts advocating abortion, and it left a horrible taste in my mouth. I finally asked Seth why he wanted his own Abort73 shirt so badly and if he knew what they were all about. His five-year-old answer was far more lucid than many of the teens and adults I've dealt with, and I no longer had any concerns about letting him wear Abort73.

In light of Seth and Melanie's childhood, I have often tried to recall my first exposure to abortion. I have never been able to pin it down. My earliest memory of the subject goes back to the ninth grade. Sitting in Mr. Rennie's English class at my Christian high school, one of my classmates complained that she didn't see any reason why a Christian couldn't support abortion. I don't remember what led to that statement or how Mr. Rennie responded, but I remember being furious at her suggestion. I quickly concluded that if she didn't see anything wrong with abortion, she must not be a Christian.

It's easy to write off my swift conclusion as the narrow and naive ideology of a sheltered 14-year-old, but what do we do with the similar remarks of a much more authoritative 72-year-old? I recently saw a video interview of R.C. Sproul, marking the 20th anniversary and re-release of his book, *Abortion: A Rational Look at an Emotional Issue*. Even as someone who has devoted my vocational life to combating abortion, I was struck by the force of his closing remarks. He says,

> [Abortion] is not just evil. It is a monstrous evil. I've spent my whole life studying theology, teaching theology, and I can tell you, if I know anything at all about God, I know that God hates abortion, and I know that he will not tolerate this forever.[1]

R.C. Sproul is one of the most respected, articulate, and studied theologians in America. He has more than 70 books to his name, and he is essentially saying, *If I'm wrong on this point, if I'm wrong about God's utter hatred for abortion, then I'm wrong about everything else.* "If I know anything at all about God, I know that God hates abortion." That is a staggering proclamation—especially when we consider again that the word abortion never appears in the Bible.

The purpose of chapter one was to demonstrate that God is not pro-abortion. The purpose of chapter two is to demonstrate that God hates abortion. As a ninth-grade English student, I was angry at the assertion that Christians should be free to have or support an abortion. As it turns out, anger is the only proper response to such a suggestion. If I have been guilty of anything, I have been guilty of not being angry enough. Where that ninth-grade fervor came from, I can't be sure, but it's interesting to note that I had just made my first journey through the Bible in a year. Among other things,

1   Sproul, R.C. "R.C. Sproul Discusses the Issue of Abortion." Ligonier Ministries. 5 Jan. 2011. <http://vimeo.com/18468741>.

that experience put me in passages that most junior-high, Sunday school students aren't exposed to. Sunday school is good at covering the "hits." Reading through the entire Bible introduced me to the "deep tracks." These passages lack the more immediate mass-appeal of their better-known cousins, but offer glimpses of God that are crucial to the holistic understanding of his character. The terrible fury of God lives in the deep tracks.

God's hatred is not a topic that gets much ink in contemporary, evangelical circles. Some passively avoid it. Some are positively offended by it and try to distance the "loving" God of the New Testament from the "hateful" God of the Old Testament. The reason such efforts are misguided is because the love of God cannot exist apart from the hatred of God. An indifferent God could survive without hatred. A loving God cannot. While it's true that the most famous verse in all of scripture is anchored on God's love ("For God so loved the world that he gave his only begotten son..."), the hatred of God is implicit to the message. If God didn't hate sin so perfectly, so passionately, so uncompromisingly, he wouldn't have had to sacrifice his own son to remove it. He could have let it slide. The only way his love for us can be compatible with his hatred for sin is if the stain of that sin is removed. Jesus died to justify us from sin and to justify God for his mercy.[2] Had John 3:16 been rendered, "For God so hated sin that he gave his only begotten son," it would simply be expressing the other side of the same sentiment.

---

2   Romans 3:26

I like how Tim Keller addresses this connection in a sermon he delivered on Abraham's intervention for the cities of Sodom and Gomorrah.[3] He notes that many people take issue with the idea that a loving God would destroy an entire city with fire and brimstone. *I don't believe in a judging God,* they argue, *I believe in a merciful God.* What they're missing, Keller says, is that,

> if you have a God who never judges, you don't have a merciful God … if you have a merciful God who hears the cry of the oppressed, and he won't judge, then he's not merciful. You can't pit these things against each other. A God who never judges isn't merciful.

In other words, a God who doesn't hate what is actively assaulting those he loves is not really loving them. In the case of Sodom and Gomorrah, the cries of the oppressed rose up to heaven,[4] and God's love for the oppressed required judgment against the oppressors. God's hatred is the necessary counterpart to God's love.

On that note, it would be helpful to take a quick, scriptural survey on the topic of divine hatred. Our goal is to categorically identify the kinds of things God hates so we can determine whether it's fair to count abortion among the objects of God's hatred. Starting at the beginning, the earliest

---

3   Keller, Timothy "Real Friendship and the Pleading Priest." Redeemer Presbyterian Church, 3 June 2001. <http://sermons2.redeemer.com/ sermons/real-friendship-and-pleading-priest>.

4   Genesis 18:20

declaration of God explicitly hating something comes in Deuteronomy 12:31. The context is child sacrifice. Because this is a topic I want to give specific attention to, I'm going to skip to the second instance and start from there.

In Deuteronomy 16:21-22, we read that God hates idolatry. Psalm 5:5 tells us that God hates all evildoers, particularly the boastful. God hates those who love violence;[5] God hates wickedness.[6] God hates empty religiosity, marked by a lack of justice and a lack of concern for the oppressed, the fatherless, and the widow.[7] According to Isaiah 61:8, God hates robbery and wrongdoing. Jeremiah 12:8 tells us that God hated the rebellion of His people. Hosea 9:15 says the same thing. In Jeremiah 44:4, God calls Israel's service and offerings to false gods an "abomination that I hate!" Amos 5:21 reveals that God hates feasts and celebrations where injustice persists. He hates the pride and self-reliance of Israel.[8] Zechariah 8:16-17 tells us that God hates evil and false oaths.

The most difficult declaration of God's hatred is found in Malachi 1:2-3 and is repeated in Romans 9:13: "I have loved Jacob but Esau I have hated." Though we could spend a lifetime wrestling through the implications of these verses, I find the notes from the ESV Study Bible helpful: "In this context loved refers to choice rather than affection, and hated refers to rejection rather than animosity (which was explicitly prohibited against Edomites, Esau's descendants, in Deut.

5   Psalm 11:5
6   Psalm 45:7
7   Isaiah 1:14-17
8   Amos 6:8

23:7)."[9] It's also possible that Malachi's remarks refer more to the nations descended from Jacob and Esau than to the men themselves. In either case, the point of the declaration, both in Malachi and Romans, is to demonstrate that God chooses according to his own will, not according to the personal merits of those who are chosen. Perhaps the best-known declaration on the hatred of God comes from Proverbs 6:16-19:

> There are six things that the LORD hates,
> seven that are an abomination to him:
> haughty eyes, a lying tongue, and hands that
> shed innocent blood, a heart that devises
> wicked plans, feet that make haste to run to
> evil, a false witness who breathes out lies,
> and one who sows discord among brothers.

Almost all of the New Testament references to hatred are warnings that those who follow Christ will be hated by the world. Beyond the repeat reference to God's "hatred" for Esau in Romans 9:13, the author of Hebrews applies Psalm 45:7 to the Messiah. Jesus is praised for loving righteousness and hating wickedness.[10] The last explicit reference to the hatred of God is found in Revelation 2:6, where the church in Ephesus is commended for hating the work of the Nicolaitans, which God tells us, he also hates. The Bible doesn't reveal who the Nicolaitans were or what they were teaching, but they may have been followers of Nicolaus, who was made a deacon in

---

9   English Standard Version (ESV) Study Bible. (Wheaton: Crossway Bibles, 2008) 1774.

10 Hebrews 1:9

Acts 6, but later went apostate according to some historians. Whoever they were, the teachings of the Nicolaitans are referenced alongside idolatry and sexual immorality.[11]

All things considered, the scriptural list of things God hates is not a particularly long one, but the categories are broad. To summarize: God hates idolatry, pride, evil, evil doers, wickedness, violence, hands that shed innocent blood, injustice, robbery, wrongdoing, rebellion, lying, discord, and sexual immorality. Look at that list again and ask yourself whether abortion could be fairly categorized under any of the abominations mentioned. Perhaps a better question would be whether there is anything on the list that abortion could *not* be categorized under. So far as I can tell, the answer is no. It is no stretch to say that abortion has a direct connection to everything God hates. Abortion is an act of violence that sheds innocent blood. It is a wicked and unjust assault on the fatherless.[12] It robs an innocent human being of its very life. It is almost always performed on the heels of sexual immorality.[13] It is sold through lies and deceit, creating discord between mother and child. It is an act of rebellion against the authority of God, justified through arrogant, prideful claims (*My Body, My Choice!*). It makes an idol out of personal autonomy, and no matter how noble their intentions, anyone who continually destroys the most innocent and helpless members of the

---

11 Revelation 2:14-15

12 In the truest sense of the word, the victims of abortion are fatherless children. Their biological fathers are either violently antagonistic towards them or powerless to save them.

13 Eighty-four percent of all U.S. abortions are performed on unmarried women.

human community is an evil-doer of the highest order. That is why God hates abortion.

But did you notice I left one item off the scriptural list of things God hates? Chronologically, it's the first one we came to, the one I skipped over, and the only one to have a relatively narrow application: child sacrifice. Everything else on the list is a broad category of vice. This one is very specific, and God positions it as the ultimate expression of evil. This is what we read in Deuteronomy 12:29-31:

> When the Lord your God cuts off before you the nations whom you go in to dispossess, and you dispossess them and dwell in their land, take care that you be not ensnared to follow them, after they have been destroyed before you, and that you do not inquire about their gods, saying, 'How did these nations serve their gods?—that I also may do the same.' You shall not worship the Lord your God in that way, for every abominable thing that the Lord hates they have done for their gods, for they even burn their sons and their daughters in the fire to their gods.

As the Israelites prepare to enter the Promised Land, God warns them against following after the false gods of the people that he is going to strike down before them. These nations have done "every abominable thing that the Lord hates" in service to their gods. If that isn't censure enough, the warning concludes with the declaration that they are so evil, they even sacrifice their own children. Everything that God hates, everything that is an abomination to him, these people have done, but the only specific act Moses singles out, through the leading of the Holy Spirit, is child sacrifice. It stands over and above every other act of depravity. We see this again in 2 Kings 16:1-3, when the author describes King Ahaz as being so evil that "he even burned his son as an offering." In Jeremiah 7:30-31, God declares through his prophet why he has rejected his people. We read:

> For the sons of Judah have done evil in my sight, declares the Lord. They have set their detestable things in the house that is called by my name, to defile it. And they have built the high places of Topheth, which is in the Valley of the Son of Hinnom, to burn their sons and their daughters in the fire, which I did not command, nor did it come into my mind.

Here again, child sacrifice is singled out as the pinnacle expression of evil. And then the condemnation gets even stronger. God declares: *not only did I not command child sacrifice, but it never even entered my mind!* The same sentiment is expressed at the end of Jeremiah 19: 3-5:

> You shall say, 'Hear the word of the Lord, O kings of Judah and inhabitants of Jerusalem. Thus says the Lord of hosts, the God of

Israel: Behold, I am bringing such disaster upon this place that the ears of everyone who hears of it will tingle. Because the people have forsaken me and have profaned this place by making offerings in it to other gods whom neither they nor their fathers nor the kings of Judah have known; and because they have filled this place with the blood of innocents, and have built the high places of Baal to burn their sons in the fire as burnt offerings to Baal, which I did not command or decree, nor did it come into my mind.

We find it again in Jeremiah 32:35. God never commanded Israel to kill their children, nor did it even enter his mind. There are a couple ways to interpret this. Either it never entered God's mind that his people could commit such an atrocity, or it never entered God's mind to command such an atrocity. If the first, clearly it's a figurative declaration, since God knows everything and is taken surprise by nothing. He's already warned Israel against child sacrifice, but perhaps he meant to shock them with the assertion that child sacrifice is so evil, the all-knowing mind of God couldn't even imagine it to be possible. If the second interpretation is correct, we learn that God never had the slightest notion to allow for the sacrificing of children. The practice is so contrary to his character that it never entered his mind to endorse it.

Child sacrifice turns up again in Psalm 106, which provides a recounting of Israel's cyclic rebellion. It is both a confession of collective guilt and a testament of God's grace and forgiveness. It begins with Israel's failure to trust God at the Red Sea and chronicles their growing expressions of sin in the desert, including their demand for meat, their rebellion against Moses, and their worship of the golden calf. After each act of rebellion, God's anger is kindled, but mercy prevails. For the sake of his name and often through the intervention of a faithful servant, God's wrath is abated. And then we get to verses 34-42. After entering the Promised Land and failing to destroy the wicked people God had commanded them to, Israel "mixed with the nations and learned to do as they did." The final act listed in this record of grievances reads as follows:

> They sacrificed their sons and their daughters
> to the demons; they poured out innocent
> blood, the blood of their sons and daughters,
> whom they sacrificed to the idols of Canaan,
> and the land was polluted with blood.

According to this account, the last straw for Israel was the sacrificing of their own children to foreign idols. Continuing to read, we find God's response in verses 40-42:

> Then the anger of the Lord was kindled
> against his people, and he abhorred his
> heritage; he gave them into the hand of the
> nations, so that those who hated them ruled
> over them. Their enemies oppressed them,

> and they were brought into subjection under
> their power.

God's patience carried Israel through forty years of desert wanderings. It had been tested and tried, but through it all, God protected Israel from their enemies. And then they started killing their children. God's hand of protection was removed, and Israel was given over to the nations who hated them. Can there be any conclusion but that God bears a unique and severe hatred for child sacrifice? And make no mistake, this is precisely what abortion is. Every single one sacrifices an innocent child to a false, demon god. When I first began combating abortion as a full-time vocation, I was directed to an abortion cover story in *New Age Journal*.[14] The author calmly asserts that abortion is a religious sacrament. She cites the book, *Pagan Meditations* by Ginette Paris, who says that it is only when we see abortion as "a sacred sacrifice to Artemis" that the sanctity of the aborted life is restored. The author dreams of the day when all daughters will be initiated into the "spiritual dignity" of abortion, "with prayers to Artemis or the Divine Mother, She who gives and takes life." Unable to convince herself that her own abortion was an immaterial procedure, she finds comfort in counting it a sacrifice to the Divine Mother, and asks that "the spirit of this, my child, [may] come again—when the world and when I welcome its rebirth."

---

14 Brenda Peterson, *The Abortion Debate: Can We Find Common Ground?* (New Age Journal, October 1993).

Though most aborting women don't have it in their minds that they're sacrificing their child to a pagan goddess, virtually every abortion is performed in service to a false god. We may not worship stone statues, but we are surrounded by the idols of money, power, prestige, autonomy, and sex. Abortion after abortion is laid down at the feet of these gods. And the true God sees every one, which is worth considering in its own right. The only way for massive, violent injustices to survive is for the perpetrators to keep them hidden. The reason an entire nation of "decent" people isn't outraged by abortion is because we don't see it. The "pro-choice" lobby works hard to keep abortion out of the limelight, and the womb itself is an intrinsically concealed place. Truly, abortion is as hidden an injustice as there has ever been. In most instances, it's a blind procedure; even the abortionist doesn't see what he's doing. But God sees every one. Our frame was not hidden from him in the womb; "No creature is hidden from his sight, but all are naked and exposed to the eyes of him to whom we must give account."[15] I first felt the weight of this while reading Gary Haugen's *Good News About Injustice*. He writes this:

> In Rwanda, where I had to bear the burden of digging through the twisted, reeking remains of horrific mass graves, I tried to imagine for just a minute, what it must have been like for God to be present at each of the massacre sites as thousands of Tutsi women and

15 Hebrews 4:13

children were murdered. Frankly, the idea was impossible to bear. But the thought led me to imagine what it must be like for God to be present, this year, at the rape of all the world's child prostitutes, at the beatings of all the world's prisoners of conscience, at the moment the last breath of hope expires from the breast of each of the millions of small children languishing in slavery. As I would approach my God in prayer, I could hear his gentle voice saying to me, "Son, do you have any idea where your Father has been lately?"[16]

I would add to that list abortion. You and I are protected from its stench by a chasm of separation. God is not. In reading through all the biblical inclusions of the word "hate," I came upon a shockingly grotesque passage in Micah 3. It reads as follows:

> Hear, you heads of Jacob and rulers of the house of Israel! Is it not for you to know justice?—you who hate the good and love the evil, who tear the skin from off my people and their flesh from off their bones, who eat the flesh of my people, and flay their skin from off them, and break their bones in

16 Haugen, Gary. *Good News About Injustice, Updated 10th Anniversary Edition: A Witness of Courage in a Hurting World.* (Downer's Grove: IVP Books, 2009) 95.

> pieces and chop them up like meat in a pot,
> like flesh in a cauldron.

Surely this is symbolic speech—meant to expose the depravity of their wicked hearts by attributing to them the most physically depraved acts one could possibly imagine. For who would actually tear the skin off their victims, or flay the skin from their bones? Who would break their bones in pieces or chop them up like meat in a pot, like flesh in a cauldron? Such behavior is unthinkable, and yet this is precisely what abortion does. If you have never seen it's violent aftermath, this is where you put the book down, visit Abort73.com and go to "Photographic Evidence." It's time to be shocked and horrified. But as shocking and horrifying as these images are, they are nothing compared with what it must be like to actually be in the womb as these tiny bodies are literally ripped apart. This is what God sees, thousands of times a day—the most innocent and helpless members of his most prized creation torn to shreds. Can you imagine his fury? Can you imagine what it will be like when the floodgates of God's wrath finally open in response to the injustice of abortion?

To this, some will raise an objection. If God is physically present for every abortion, if his anger burns at every one, why doesn't he act to stop them? We'll wrestle through that question at the book's conclusion. For now, I'll offer two responses. The first is Paul's—offered in the context of God's choosing Jacob over Esau.[17] Who are we to question

---

17 Romans 9:14-24

the wisdom or goodness of God? Does clay have the right to question the potter? Second, I would suggest that abortion is both deserving of God's wrath and an expression of God's wrath. Romans 1 tells us that those who suppress the truth of God, truth that is revealed to everyone through the created order and the human conscience, will eventually be given over to their sinful desires. Verse 28 explains that, "since they did not see fit to acknowledge God, God gave them up to a debased mind to do what ought not to be done." Those who continue to rebel against the authority of God will eventually get their wish. God will give them over to everything they want, and it will destroy them. It is only the mercy of God that spares us from our warped desires. When we are given over to pursue our "dishonorable passions" the results are socially devastating: "envy, murder, strife, deceit, maliciousness… men committing shameless acts with men and receiving in themselves the due penalty for their error." Some see God's commandments as narrow, arbitrary and inhibiting. In reality, they are a protection. When we abandon them, things go terribly wrong. In the case of abortion, we kill children in pursuit of a happier future and in the process, we destroy our future, we destroy our families, we destroy our culture, we destroy our consciences, and we destroy our peace. We want God to leave us alone, and so he does—which is a judgment in itself.

The more important question for us is not what stays God's hand, but what stays ours. Francis Chan observes that when we question God as to why he allows so many people to die of starvation, God "has more of a right to ask us why so many people are starving."[18] He's God. He's answerable to no one. He created a perfect world with abundant, ready-made food for everyone. It was our sin that broke the system. It is selfishness and greed that keeps people starving today, not a lack of food. But what about abortion? Do we hate it as God does, or are we indifferent to abortion or even thankful for it? It seems as if many in the church consider it merciful or progressive to tolerate abortion, to exhibit no zeal for the issue—as if God is honored by indifference to this abominable injustice. If that is true, it would be good to remind ourselves of a couple things.

Jesus tells us in Matthew 10:24 that "a disciple is not above his teacher, nor a servant above his master." He continues, "It is enough for the disciple to be like his teacher, and the servant like his master. If they have called the master of the house Beelzebul, how much more will they malign those of his household." In other words, we shouldn't expect or aspire to a better reputation than Christ. If God consistently identifies child sacrifice as the most egregious of human sins, should we do less? Or are we more enlightened than our Creator? And lest you argue that Christ never exhibited the same fervor over child sacrifice as the Father, remember the singularity of purpose that exists between the two. And remember that Jesus was indignant at the mere suggestion that children were insignificant. What would his response have been if they were being killed?! He rebukes the disciples for shooing children away,[19] commands that no one "despise" a

---

18 Chan, Francis. *Crazy Love*. (Colorado Springs, David C. Cook, 2008) 31.
19 Matthew 19:14, Mark 10:14, Luke 18:16

child,[20] and says whoever receives a child in his name, receives himself.[21] In light of such statements, is there any possibility Jesus takes a sympathetic view of abortion—an institution that is intrinsically built on the disregard of children? And in case you hold the view that Jesus takes a gentler view of things than his Father, consider Christ's words in John 5:19: "Truly, truly, I say to you, the Son can do nothing of his own accord, but only what he sees the Father doing. For whatever the Father does, that the Son does likewise."

You might say God the Father and God the Son are connected at the hip. Everything that is important to the Father is important to the Son. Jesus came to affirm and uphold everything the Father commanded.[22] He says to us, "whoever does the will of my Father in heaven is my brother and sister and mother."[23] Ask yourself, is tolerating or turning a blind eye to child sacrifice the will of the Father? Doesn't God expect us to hate the things he hates? Scripture says he does. Proverbs 8:13 proclaims that "the fear of the Lord is the hatred of evil." Psalm 111:10, Proverbs 1:7, and Proverbs 9:10 all tell us that the fear of the Lord is the beginning of wisdom. Put them together and you get: *The hatred of evil is the beginning of wisdom.* Psalm 97:10 commands those who love the Lord, to "hate evil!" Amos 5:15 commands us to "hate evil, and love good." All that to say, we should not be embarrassed or apologetic about hating abortion. Rather, we should be embarrassed if we *don't* hate abortion.

---

20 Matthew 18:10

21 Mark 9:37, Luke 9:48

22 Matthew 5:17, Luke 16:17

23 Matthew 12:50

The word abortion may never appear on the pages of Scripture, but child-sacrifice does. And God hates it. God hates child sacrifice. But because abortion has been so commonplace for so long, and because so many in the church have simply grown up with it, we've demonstrated almost no capacity to mirror God's hatred for it. Those who support abortion don't mind its existence; those who oppose abortion don't want to be bothered by it. Both responses are prompted by a grossly inadequate understanding of what is actually happening. As we bring this chapter to a close, stop and think about the fact that in the United States of America, it is legal to dissect and dismember the most innocent, helpless members of the human community. We do it thousands of times a day as God watches every one. It's time we asked him for the grace to hate abortion more.

Chapter Three

THE SECULAR CASE AGAINST ABORTION

I CAN'T SAY FOR CERTAIN, but I believe my first exposure to anti-abortion activism came toward the end of my high school career, somewhere around 1994. I was part of the student ministries at Grace Community Church in Sun Valley, CA, and as I crossed the street to get to service one Sunday, there were a handful of people on the sidewalk with pictures of aborted children. If I remember correctly, they were criticizing our pastor for not doing more to combat abortion. It was not a pleasant experience, and though I passed by without engaging, I was quick to rally to the mental defense of my church. It wasn't hard to convince myself that these people were completely out of touch. Everyone at Grace already knew that abortion was wrong. Why not save their ire for someone else?!

Looking back, I wish I could remember more details. How did these "protesters" carry themselves? Were they friendly? Did they yell? Did my annoyance owe to the pictures, to their demeanor, or to the mere fact that the normal flow of my Sunday was interrupted? I can recall the place perfectly, the northwest corner of Roscoe and Nagle, but almost everything else escapes me. Nevertheless, I learned a lesson that morning that has followed me ever since: those who actively oppose abortion can be a real nuisance! I say that neither to their credit nor shame. As someone who has now spent more than ten years on the activist side, I can sympathize with those holding the signs *and* with those trying to avoid them. I've devoted my vocational life to combating abortion, but in many ways, I remain as wary and skeptical of pro-life activism as ever. How easy it is to combat unhealthy indifference with unhealthy obsession.

For the record, I was wrong about abortion in high school. I was wrong to blankly condemn the sign-holders on that Sunday morning, and I was wrong to simply write them off. I called myself "pro-life," but like so many others, I was ignorant and confused. I didn't want to deal with the ugliness and awkwardness of abortion, so it was much easier to just criticize those who did. As it turns out, I wasn't the only one selling the case against abortion short—not by a long shot. In the years to come, I would realize that the divide over abortion is not primarily an ethical one. It's an *educational* one. Anyone who believes it's wrong to kill a baby already has the moral framework necessary to condemn abortion. What most people lack is a basic, biological understanding of prenatal development. Many who call themselves "pro-choice" have simply defaulted to that position because the evidence against abortion has never been presented to them—not in the classroom, not in the clinic, and not in most churches.

Abort73.com was created to fill an educational void. Today, it is no stretch to say that Abort73 offers the most comprehensive, engaging, and accessible abortion education in the world—available around the clock and around the globe to anyone who can get online. I have no intention of recreating the Abort73 website over the course of this chapter (nor could I), but I do want to draw your attention to some of the basic, biological reasons for opposing abortion. Why? Because the arguments I made in the first two chapters become exponentially stronger when you understand the basic biology of prenatal development. If you're hesitant to apply Scripture's condemnation of child sacrifice to embryos and fetuses, this should cure you.

Before I got involved with the abortion issue vocationally, my biggest misconception centered on the question of life's beginning. As it turns out, there's no question at all. The precise beginning of individual human life has long been a biologically settled fact. Life begins at conception, which means that every single abortion, at every stage of pregnancy kills a genetically distinct human being. If you visit the first page in Abort73's Case Against Abortion, you'll find a staggering amount of testimony affirming this. Current and past medical texts, National Geographic videos, world-renowned doctors and geneticists, prominent "pro-choice" ethicists, a former Planned-Parenthood president, and even the physician who co-founded NARAL all testify to the fact that every abortion kills a living human being. There is no debate on this point. But like so many others, I had bought into the all-too-common notion that "nobody knows when life begins"—a confusion that permeates all the way to the Supreme Court. When Justice Harry Blackmun wrote the majority opinion for Roe vs. Wade, the decision that made abortion a federally protected act, he explicitly appeals to the supposed uncertainty of life's beginning. He writes:

> The judiciary, at this point in the development of man's knowledge, is not in a position to... resolve the difficult question of when life begins... since those trained in the respective disciplines of medicine, philosophy, and theology are unable to arrive at any consensus.[1]

Justice Blackmun's statement is patently false. Philosophers and theologians may debate life's beginning, but those in medicine do not. Bernard Nathanson is the New York physician who co-founded NARAL and directed the largest abortion clinic in the country during the run-up to *Roe*. At its peak, his clinic performed 100 abortions a day, seven days a week. He had this to say about *Roe vs. Wade*:

> Of course, I was pleased with Justice Harry Blackmun's abortion decisions, which were an unbelievably sweeping triumph for our cause, far broader than our 1970 victory in New York or the advances since then. I was pleased with Blackmun's conclusions, that is. I could not plumb the ethical or medical

1   Roe v. Wade, 410 U.S. 113. Supreme Court of the United States. 1973.

> reasoning that had produced the conclusions.
> Our final victory had been propped up on a
> misreading of obstetrics, gynecology, and
> embryology, and that's a dangerous way to
> win.[2]

Nathanson calls Blackmun's "regrettably ill-informed" assertion that those in medicine do not know when life begins the "crucial flaw in the decision."[3] Some years later, a U.S. Senate Judiciary Subcommittee would conclude that, "Physicians, biologists, and other scientists agree that conception marks the beginning of the life of a human being—a being that is alive and is a member of the human species. There is overwhelming agreement on this point in countless medical, biological, and scientific writings."[4] Nathanson further notes that "the basics [of prenatal development] were well-known to human embryology at the time the U.S. Supreme Court issued its 1973 rulings, even though the rulings made no use of them."[5] What are some of those basics? If you visit Abort73's "Prenatal Development" page, you'll learn among other things that the heart starts beating 21 days after conception. Four days later, it will be pumping blood throughout the embryo's tiny body—beating approximately 54 million times before birth. During week four, the brain begins dividing into its three primary sections and the arms

2   Nathanson, M.D., Bernard N, *Aborting America*. (New York: Pinnacle Books, 1979) 163.

3   Nathanson, 211.

4   Report, Subcommittee on Separation of Powers to Senate Judiciary Committee S-158, 97th Congress, 1st Session 1981, 7.

5   Report, 201.

and legs take shape. Hands and feet emerge after four weeks. After six weeks, the brain emits measurable brain impulses, and the embryo responds reflexively to stimulus and may be able to feel pain. Distinct leg movements and hiccups have been observed after seven weeks. Fingers and toes are now separated and the embryo develops the ability to smell. After eight weeks, every organ is present and in place—though the baby (now called a fetus) is less than two inches long. At nine weeks, fetuses are capable of sucking their thumb, grasping objects, responding to touch, and doing somersaults.

Even abortion-advocating law experts generally admit that *Roe vs. Wade* is an extremely confused and largely indefensible ruling. One such critic is a former clerk to Justice Blackmun, Edward Lazaurs. He affirms that he "loved Roe's author like a grandfather," is "utterly committed to the right to choose," but counts *Roe vs. Wade* as "the most damaging of judicial decisions." This clerk turned federal prosecutor writes:

> What, exactly, is the problem with *Roe*? The problem, I believe, is that it has little connection to the Constitutional right it purportedly interpreted… [W]hen Democratic senators oppose a judicial appointment because of the nominee's opposition to *Roe*, they not only endorse but make a litmus test out of one of the most intellectually suspect constitutional decisions of the modern era. They practically

> require that a judicial nominee sign on to
> logic that is, at best, questionable, and at
> worst, disingenuous and results-oriented.[6]

Whether Blackmun's verdict helped drive the cultural confusion regarding life's beginning or was simply a result of it, the net effect is the same. Despite overwhelming medical consensus, it's still fairly common to hear the knee-jerk, "it's not a baby yet" argument. The same claim is made inside most abortion clinics, where no one is around to take them to task. But the more honest and informed abortion advocates must appeal to an increasingly sophisticated (and sinister) argument if they're to retain any credibility. It grants the existence of individual human life in the womb and accepts that a real death is taking place, but argues that abortion still serves the greater good. How? By sparing children from lives of suffering and freeing up resources for the needs of those already born. As it becomes increasingly difficult to deny the humanity of children in the womb, this is the line of reasoning more and more abortion advocates are taking up. As to the first claim, this idea that abortion is a legitimate means of sparing children from being born into a life of neglect, it is grossly presumptive. It assumes a life of suffering on the child and assumes that this suffering will be a fate worse than death. Though it's hard to imagine even the staunchest abortion advocate suggesting that we kill

---

6   Lazarus, Edward. "The Lingering Problems With Roe v. Wade, And Why
     the Recent Senate Hearings on Michael Mcconnell's Nomination Only
     Underlined Them." *FindLaw*. Thomson Reuters, 3 Oct. 2002. <http://writ.
     news.findlaw.com/lazarus/20021003.html>.

born children as a means of eliminating potential suffering, Planned Parenthood's founder, Margaret Sanger, once said, "the most merciful thing that a large family does to one of its infant members is to kill it."[7]

Towards the end of my collegiate career, I read Toni Morrison's Pulitzer Prize winning novel, *Beloved*. The central character in the story is a runaway slave mother who, on the verge of recapture, slits the throat of her daughter to prevent her from reentering a life of slavery. I don't know that I saw the connection to abortion at the time, but I have since reread the text in pursuit of the details I'd forgotten. Though I don't know Morrison's position on abortion, I found her account of this mercy killing far less sympathetic than I anticipated. After killing her daughter, Sethe is shunned by her own people—the very ones with first-hand knowledge of what she was trying to protect her child from. Her sons run away forever, terrified by what their mother had done. Baby Suggs, the town matriarch and Sethe's mother-in-law, loses all hope, shuts herself up in her room, and dies. Beloved, the young daughter who was killed, haunts the family in a perennial fury until she finally shows up in bodily form to torment and almost kill her mother. Near the end of the book, we find this account of Sethe's efforts to justify her actions to Beloved:

> Sethe began to talk, explain, describe how much she had suffered, been through, for her children... None of which made the

---

7   Sanger, Margaret. *Woman and the New Race.* (New York: Brentano's, 1920) Chapter V. <http://www.bartleby.com/1013/5.html>.

impression it was supposed to. Beloved accused her of leaving her behind... And Sethe cried, saying she never did, or meant to—that she had to get them out, away... That her plan was always that they would all be together on the other side, forever. Beloved wasn't interested. She said when she cried there was no one... Sethe pleaded for forgiveness, counting, listing again her reasons: that Beloved was more important, meant more to her than her own life. That she would trade places any day. Give up her life, every minute and hour of it, to take back one of Beloved's tears.[8]

As bad as slavery was, what Sethe did was worse. When she tried to convince another former slave there was no other way, he simply stated, "There could have been a way. Some other way... You got two feet, Sethe, not four."[9]   Human beings are image bearers. We are not animals. We have two feet, not four. We do not eliminate suffering by killing those who suffer. Though the focus of this chapter is on the secular reasons for condemning abortion, the front line arguments in support of abortion are almost all spiritual in nature—despite the fact that they're being made by secularists. Their goal is to move the debate away from objective, measurable criteria so as to place it in a realm that science and biology can't

---

8   Morrison, Toni. *Beloved*. (New York: Alfred A. Knopf, 1987) 241-242.

9   Morrison, Toni. 165.

speak to. In it's crudest form, they are arguing that abortion-vulnerable children are better off dead. To demonstrate just how deplorable this "mercy killing" mentality is, we must return to Scripture. The Bible does not paint a kind picture of suicide, which is a self-inflicted mercy killing. How much worse are those who kill *others* in the name of benevolence?

The final chapter of I Samuel records the death of King Saul. When he was mortally wounded in battle, Saul commanded his armor-bearer to, "Draw your sword, and thrust me through with it, lest these uncircumcised come and thrust me through, and mistreat me."[10] If there was ever an appropriate place for a mercy killing, surely this was it. But Saul's armor bearer feared to lift his hand against God's anointed and would not do it. In 2 Samuel 1:1-15, the news of Saul's death is brought to David through an Amalekite witness. Because the details from the 2 Samuel account don't quite match those from the I Samuel account, there are two possible conclusions. Either Saul's attempt to kill himself was unsuccessful and the Amalekite finished the job at Saul's bidding, or as is more generally believed, the Amalekite was lying to gain David's favor. In either case, the material point is unchanged. Despite the general consensus that Saul "could not live after he had fallen,"[11] David had the Amalekite executed on the spot for thinking it commendable to put Saul out of his misery. This text gives no credence to the idea that killing someone is a morally legitimate means of sparing them from future suffering.

---

10 I Samuel 31:4
11 2 Samuel 1:10

In a scenario that has striking parallels to the deaths of Saul and his son, Jonathan, J.R.R. Tolkien offers insight through the words of Gandalf in his conclusion to the *Lord of the Rings* trilogy. The Lord of Gondor, mad with despair at the pending fall of his kingdom and the condition of his dying, unconscious son, has commanded his men to set them both on fire. He believes it will be more honorable to die together, on his own terms, than at the hands of a cruel and merciless enemy. To that Gandalf says: "Authority is not given to you, Steward of Gondor, to order the hour of your death. And only the heathen kings, under the domination of the Dark Power, did thus, slaying themselves in pride and despair, murdering their kin to ease their own death."[12] Taking a life, even one that is suffering anguish with little hope of survival, is a grave and serious thing. At its core, it's a prideful thing. Those who take such steps thumb their noses at the sovereign designs of God *through* suffering and set themselves up as the ultimate authority over their life or the life of another.

Returning to the more specific context of abortion, the second half of the "greater good" argument says that even if abortion kills one life, it can still have a positive impact on all life. It's a cost/benefit assessment, which believes abortion's benefit to the collective supersedes its cost to the individual. For us to accept such a conclusion, recognizing again that this is an intrinsically spiritual argument, we must be able to find biblical examples of God granting the authority to usurp the life or liberty of an individual human being for the

---

12 J.R.R. Tolkien, *The Return of the King* (Boston: Houghton Mifflin Company, 1955) 835.

mutual benefit of all human beings. As I thought through this question, I was able to come up with lots of examples where the interests of the collective are superseded for the sake of the one, but you almost never see it go the other way. Consider the Parable of the Lost Sheep: "What man of you, having a hundred sheep, if he has lost one of them, does not leave the ninety-nine in the open country, and go after the one that is lost, until he finds it?"[13] The safety of the 99 is compromised so that the shepherd can look for the one. Wouldn't it have been of more benefit to the 99 to leave the one behind?

Even more remarkable is the immediate context of this parable in Matthew's account. Matthew 18 opens with the disciples asking Jesus who is the greatest in the kingdom of heaven. Jesus immediately calls a child to him and sets the child in their midst. He says, "unless you turn and become like children, you will never enter the kingdom of heaven." He then says if you receive a child, you receive me (v. 5), but if you cause a child to sin, you would have been better off dead (v. 6). Continuing to verse 10, Jesus warns against despising a little child, and here's his reason: "For I tell you that in heaven their angels always see the face of my Father who is in heaven." The implication is that each child has an angel who has constant and direct access to God the Father. If you mistreat that child, you can be rest assured that God will hear about it. Following this warning, Jesus tells the parable of the lost sheep to illustrate what he means in saying, "do not despise one of these little ones." The shepherd who leaves one sheep to go astray so he can stay with the 99 despises

13 Luke 15:4

that sheep. And the person who discounts one child in light of the 99 despises that child. It's that simple. Jesus concludes by saying, "it is not the will of my Father who is in heaven that one of these little ones should perish" (v. 14). If you're looking for an abortion-related theme verse, they don't get much better (or clearer) than that.

Now let's turn our attention to Genesis. When the angels of the Lord are sent to destroy the cities of Sodom and Gomorrah, Abraham pleads with them on behalf of the righteous. The angels finally declare that if they can find even ten righteous people there, the cities will not be destroyed.[14] As it turns out, there weren't ten, but the one righteous man, Lot, and his family are given a passage of escape. Generations before, when "every intention of the thoughts of [man's] heart [were] only evil continually," God did not wipe out the one righteous man, Noah, in his fury against the nations.[15] The life of the one is not compromised for the sake of the whole. When Abraham and Sarah sinned against Abimelech by telling him they were simply brother and sister, God made all the women in Abimelech's household barren.[16] When Moses sent the 12 spies into the Promised Land, the entire nation of Israel suffers for the unbelief of the 10—though the lives of the two spies who *did* believe are spared from God's collective judgment.[17] When Achan kept what was not lawful

---

14 Genesis 18:32
15 Genesis 6:5
16 Genesis 20:17
17 Numbers 14:20-25

to keep, after the defeat of Jericho, the entire Israelite army was routed in their next battle at Ai.[18]

Most significantly, through the sin of one man, all of humanity stands condemned.[19] The Bible can easily offend the western world's hypersensitivity to fairness and equality, but notice where the inequality lies. Do the scales tip towards the aggregate or towards the individual? The collective often has to suffer for the one, but not vice versa. Except once. Except on the cross. This is the only legitimate mercy killing we see in the Bible, and though Christ's death was in accordance with God's redemptive plan, the behavior of those who nailed him to the tree was certainly not justified. The nations may be blessed for the righteousness of the one or suffer for the sin of the one, but there is no legitimate precedent for killing the one to bless the nations.

In chapter two, I appealed to Scripture's singular condemnation of child sacrifice to argue that abortion is the ultimate expression of evil in the world today. It is the absolute antithesis of the greatest commandment—to love your God and love your neighbor. If intentionally killing your neighbor (who was made in the image of God!) is the ultimate expression of hatred, how much more depraved is it to kill a neighbor who has no capacity for self-defense and has never committed a single grievance against you or anyone else in the universe? That is abortion. Now I'd like to argue the same point—that abortion is the ultimate expression

---

18 Joshua 7:1
19 Romans 5:12

of evil, without appealing to the Bible. To do that, I need to point our collective memory to 9/11.

As I write this, the ten-year anniversary of the September 11 terrorist attacks is just around the corner. For many Americans, the events of that morning represent the epitome of evil. But abortion is worse. And we only need consider what made 9/11 such an atrocity to understand why. Almost 3,000 Americans were killed by the attacks on 9/11, but it's not primarily the number of people who died which makes that day so hard to stomach. It's the fact that they were unsuspecting civilians. It's devastating enough to lose 3,000 soldiers in battle, but incalculably worse to lose 3,000 innocent non-combatants, who were completely unprepared and incapable of defending themselves. For those trapped in the World Trade Center, it was death by fire or death by falling. There was no warning, and nothing they could do to stop it.

But now imagine that those terrorist attacks didn't just happen one day ten years ago. Imagine they have happened every day since, and every day for the 30 years prior to September 11, 2001. Three thousand deaths a day, times 365 days, times 40 years. Now imagine that those attacks weren't directed at corporate America or the Pentagon, but were aimed squarely at American children. What if those planes were daily crashing into pre-schools instead of sky-scrapers? Would our outrage be more or less? And what if foreign terrorists were to level their violence upon American newborns, lying in wait in maternity wards across the country, killing more than 3,000 newborns every day? Would we solace ourselves with the thought that *they're just babies, they don't even know what's happening?* What if these terrorists got even more aggressive and started killing babies before they were born? What if they were able to tranquilize the mother and then use barbarous methods to pull the arms and legs of their children off, while they were still alive!? Now imagine that those perpetrating the violence weren't foreign terrorists but fellow Americans. Or worse yet, imagine that it wasn't a nameless stranger assailing these children. Imagine these butchers were being hired by the babies' mothers to destroy their own children. And imagine that instead of intervening, the United States government sanctioned such behavior under the guise that it was a reasonable expression of freedom and equality. Though this may seem an absurd and unthinkable progression of thought, this is precisely what abortion is doing. For close to forty years, between 3,300 and 4,400[20] innocent and helpless human beings have been killed each day in the United States. Most of them are torn limb from limb, with their mother's full (if reluctant) consent. The daily death toll has exceeded 9/11 thousands of times over, claiming more than 50 million human lives in the process.

At this point, perhaps you'd like to argue that the nearly 3,000 American citizens who were killed on 9/11 were categorically more valuable than the 3,000+ American babies that are daily killed by abortion. Or perhaps you feel it is unfair or insensitive to compare these two atrocities against

---

20 Jones, Rachel K, and Kathryn Kooistra. "Abortion Incidence and Access to Services In the United States, 2008." *Perspectives on Sexual and Reproductive Health* 43:1. 10 Jan. 2011. <http://onlinelibrary.wiley.com/doi/10.1363/4304111/abstract>.

each other. If that's your concern, I would simply suggest that it is only in comparing abortion to more broadly recognized atrocities that we can fully demonstrate and understand its gravity. Historically, there are numerous infamies that are far more comparable to abortion than 9/11—which was a one-time massacre, universally condemned by the Western world, against recognized human victims. By contrast, abortion is a legal, sustained assault against a victim class that is generally considered "sub-human." Sound familiar? It should. Virtually every "genocide" in history has these traits in common.

The reason that so many people take offense at comparing abortion to past crimes against humanity is the same reason that the white establishment was scandalized when Dr. Martin Luther King Jr. compared the abuse of black Americans to the Holocaust. It is easy to condemn crimes that are far away or happened long ago; it is much harder to condemn them when they sit right in your backyard. Abortion supporters are infuriated at the notion that abortion is comparable to the Holocaust because they incessantly argue that the unborn aren't people. This is exactly the same argument that is always made to justify crimes against humanity: *They're not really people.* The language that Hitler used to dehumanize European Jews is much the same language that is used today to dehumanize children in the womb. If we can't compare atrocities past to atrocities present, then the term "never again" loses all meaning.

Twenty years ago, Stephen Schwarz developed the acronym, SLED,[21] to demonstrate that there are no qualitative differences between human beings inside the womb and human beings outside the womb. It's a helpful device for understanding the moral equivalence of killing someone in an abortion clinic and killing someone in a gas chamber. Schwarz points out that all the reasons people give for why unborn human beings are morally inferior to born human beings fit into one of four categories: Size, Level of development, Environment, and Degree of dependency. More importantly, each of these differences shows up outside the womb as well, without any bearing on basic human rights. In other words, small people aren't less human than big people, and those who are less mentally or physically developed are no less human than the more developed. Humanity doesn't stop or start depending on your location, and dependence upon outside supports has no bearing on humanity. SLED is covered in more detail on the Abort73 website, but you should already see how it applies to the Holocaust.

The fact that those killed by abortion are generally less developed and more dependent than those killed in Nazi Germany doesn't change anything. Was the murder of an estimated 1.5 Jewish children any more justified than the murder of their parents? Of course not. And though it is a mercy of God that so many abortions seem to precede rational consciousness, does that make the act any less condemnable? Is there an ethical difference between murdering a man who's

---

21 Schwarz, Stephen D. *The Moral Question of Abortion*. (Chicago: Loyola Press, 1990)

asleep and murdering a man who's awake? Were the deaths of Jewish newborns any less heinous because they weren't fully aware of what was happening? Some will say that the reason it's worse to kill people after they're born is because they have memories and life experiences. They have loved and been loved—which makes their death worse. But does it? Who loses more when they're killed? An eighty-five-year-old or a fifty-five-year-old, or a 25-year-old? How about a 15-year-old or a 5-year-old? Doesn't the man who is killed earlier lose more than the man who is killed later? And think about the impact on future generations. If someone had killed me ten years ago, my children wouldn't exist. Being murdered then would have cost far more than if I were murdered today. Make no mistake, aborted embryos and fetuses lose more of their future than anyone.

To this, some will say that comparing abortion to the Holocaust completely misses the fact that the Holocaust was a state-mandated, extermination effort. Abortion is a matter of personal choice. *If you're against abortion, you don't have to have one.* Here again, history has an answer. Slaveholders in the South justified slavery with the same "pro-choice" arguments. Nobody was forcing anyone to own slaves. If you morally objected to the practice, you could simply abstain, without expecting everyone else to embrace your same ideals. People were free to make their own choices. *After all, you can't legislate morality.* Or how about this one, unless you can take care of all the slaves that would be set free, what right do you have to criticize slavery? It's easy to see the fallacy of such arguments now, but they held incredible sway in their day. And each one was propped up on the notion that though blacks were biologically human, they were an inferior subclass of humans with nowhere near the moral significance of whites. White plantation owners may have been free to choose, but the victims of slavery were certainly not.

Tolerance is the most celebrated doctrine in the world today, but it cannot be held in the face of violent injustice. It goes from being a virtue to being a vice. We tolerate those who criticize people; we do not tolerate those who kill people. The reasons that 9/11 is condemnable are the reasons abortion is condemnable. The same goes for the Holocaust and slavery. If you need a more contemporary example, the reasons child soldiering and sex trafficking are condemnable are the same reasons abortion is condemnable. For far too long, we have been guilty of applying a baseless, double standard to the issue of abortion. Even its strongest supporters rarely frame abortion as anything less than a necessary evil—all the while reminding us that we must be tolerant of others' beliefs. But if it's wrong to tolerate terrorism or genocide, then it's wrong to tolerate abortion, whether you count yourself a Christian or not.

Chapter Four

THE RISK OF DOING NOTHING

FOR THE FIRST TWO YEARS OF OUR MARRIAGE, my wife and I lived in Orange County, CA and attended the Bible Church of Buena Park. As we headed to church one morning, something disturbing caught my eye. Turning right from Beach Boulevard onto Orangethorpe, I noticed an older man sitting on the curb—with a bloody head. As soon as I realized it was blood streaming down his face, I turned away and hoped Carrie hadn't noticed. I felt a quick pang that maybe I should do something, but the reasons for not getting involved came flooding in. *We were late for church… This man was 10 feet from a bus stop full of people... I'm not a doctor... I don't have the stomach for heavy bleeding.* And then I remembered the Good Samaritan.

I made a U-turn and drove back. The man was intoxicated and had gashed his head on the curb. None of the people at the bus stop had spoken to him or called an ambulance. I helped get him out of the street while Carrie called the paramedics from a nearby liquor store. The man could barely walk. He made it across the sidewalk and collapsed onto a narrow lawn. When the paramedics arrived, they thanked us for calling, but warned me against exposing myself to unknown blood sources—*in case I needed more reasons for not getting involved.*

Looking back, I can say with absolute certainty that, were it not for my remembrance of the Good Samaritan, I would not have turned around to help. It's easy to condemn the priest and the Levite, but in their place, I may have done the same thing. Thankfully, the story of the Good Samaritan got me to change direction that morning in California, and it got me to change vocation some years earlier in Tennessee. At its core, this simple, 6-verse narrative shatters the standard cultural understanding of who our neighbors are and what it means to love them. But before I connect the story to abortion, there are is a bigger issue to wrestle with.

The question I'd like to open with is this: What is at stake when we see a neighbor in need? What do we risk by stopping or not stopping? If I'm saved through faith, not on the basis of works, what does it matter if I stop to help a bleeding man? I read recently in a commentary on Matthew that, "it cannot be emphasized too strongly that [good deeds] are not the basis of entrance into the kingdom."[1] Though I'm happy to affirm that salvation is *not* on the basis of works, Jesus seems to constantly underemphasize this point—much as he did in the lead up to the Good Samaritan. By modern, evangelical standards, Christ was often guilty of underemphasizing belief. How many "seekers" did he turn away, without any mention

---

1   MacArthur, Jr, John F. *Matthew 24-28* (Chicago: Moody Publishers, 1989) 122.

of faith? If only Jesus could have been more theologically
articulate, like Paul! Then we wouldn't have to work so hard
to explain what he *really* meant. But here's the problem with
such silly ramblings. Paul got his theology from Jesus. More
than anyone in the universe, Jesus knows that salvation is
not (could not!) be on the basis of works. He died to take
our place, because no amount of good deeds could ever save
us! And yet he still said the things he said. Jesus Christ, God
incarnate, promises terrible things to those who don't love
their neighbor.

I am not arguing for a faith *and* works salvation anymore
than the Bible argues for a faith and works salvation. When
Paul says we're saved through faith, not as a result of works,[2]
and James says we're justified by works and not by faith alone,[3]
I believe them both—not in a postmodern sense, but in a
systematic theology sense. The statements can be reconciled
when we understand that faith in the atoning work of Christ
is the basis of our salvation, and obedience is the evidence
of our salvation. James speaks of three faiths: a dead faith,
a demon faith and a living faith. It is only a living faith that
saves, and a living faith manifests itself in obedience. We're
saved through faith alone, but saving faith is never alone.
Easy, right? Not exactly.

Theoretically, the explanation works. It harmonizes
the apparent tension we see between faith and deeds. In
real life, it never works itself out so cleanly. Here's what I
mean. If good deeds are the evidence of a living faith—the

---

2   Ephesians 2:8,9
3   James 2:24

natural outpouring of a transformed heart, I shouldn't have to manufacture them, right? The fruit of righteousness should be natural, not burdensome. But let's be honest. When I stopped to help the man on the side of the road, my underlying motive was guilt, not love. I stopped because it struck me that I'm a Christian, and this is what Christians do. That throws a wrench into the proposition I laid out above, because if the good deed doesn't come naturally, how do I know it's real? How do I know I'm not just an impostor, forcibly tweaking my external behavior to match a supposed internal change?

As it says in Matthew 12:33, "the tree is known by its fruit." Grapes are not gathered from thorn bushes; figs are not gathered from thistles. Every healthy tree bears good fruit. In fact, it *cannot* bear bad fruit.[4] The orange tree doesn't start to produce a thorn and then think, *oh wait, I'm an orange tree.* The oranges are produced naturally; it doesn't have the capacity to produce anything else. But it's not the oranges that make it an orange tree. The seed makes it an orange tree; the oranges prove what kind of seed was planted. That's how it's supposed to work in the Christian life, but there is one notable distinction.

At the point of salvation, when our heart of stone is replaced with a heart of flesh,[5] we remain in our body of sin.[6] We are redeemed, but we are not healthy in the same way a physical fruit tree is healthy, and that complicates things to no end. In the orchard, trees are known by their fruit. In

---

4   Matthew 7:16-18
5   Ezekiel 11:19
6   Romans 8:10

the church, the best we can say is that Christians are *mostly* known by their fruit. Unlike the orange tree, Christians have the capacity to produce non-Christian fruit. And non-Christians have the capacity to produce Christian-*looking* fruit. Discerning between the two is not always easy. I can look at my life and know that I am saved by faith, but I also know that the evidence of a saving faith is good fruit. And I still see a lot of bad fruit on my branches. So when I read a passage like James 2:17, or hear a sermon about the Good Samaritan, my knee-jerk reaction is to try and manufacture more fruit to show that my faith is real. But if I'm modifying my external behavior to prove an internal change has taken place, isn't that like tying oranges to the branches of a pine tree? Yes and no.

It's dangerous to attack the problem at the fruit level, but the struggle to produce fruit is often evidence that the seed has already taken root. You don't change the nature of the tree by tying fruit to the branches, but if it's a fruit tree to begin with—it is perfectly reasonable to do everything in your power to stimulate the production of as much fruit as possible. We can become so hung up on our motivation that we end up doing nothing at all. Our heart is never right in any ultimate sense; every good deed carries the taint of sin. As I made my U-turn that morning in Buena Park, I could have easily said, "You know what, I'm not doing this for the right reasons. This is not a response produced by faith and love. It's a response prompted by guilt and duty." Those would have been true sentiments, but would it have solved anything to simply leave the man bleeding in the street? Did God look on my act of service with indifference because it was not more nobly motivated? I doubt it.

I love the doctrine of Christian hedonism,[7] but I rarely live out in practice what I aspire to in theory. The Christian hedonist sees a man bleeding on the street; he knows intrinsically that it is more blessed to give than receive, and so he pursues his joy, and God's glory, by happily, heartily serving the man in need. That was very different from my experience with the bloodied man, but that doesn't cause me to abandon the pursuit. More times than not, external acts of obedience help reform my heart. My service did not begin with joy, but that's where it ended. If we take "fruit" to not only mean the good deed itself, but also the mental wrangling that gets us *to* the good deed, I think we're on the right track. The tension itself is evidence of the Spirit's work. We strive for perfect, natural obedience, but so long as we dwell in our fallen flesh, we must often employ mental exertion to convince ourselves to act rightly—even as we repent for not loving our neighbor more willingly.

In the natural order, grape vines don't produce thorns. In our case, we are grape vines that started out as thorn bushes—until God somehow infused grape seeds into our root structure. The internal grape vine is pushing itself out, but remains locked inside a thorn bush shell. As the grape seeds grow, the outer thorn bush thins. We see fewer thorns and more grapes, and the longer the process goes on, the

---

7   In its simplest form, John Piper's "doctrine of Christian hedonism" can be summed up this way: *God is most glorified in us, when we are most satisfied in him.*

easier it is to tell what kind of bush we really are. For the duration of our earthly lives, we are in process of becoming what God has declared us to be. So long as this growth in sanctification lasts, we must condition ourselves to believe that deeds matter and accept the fact that even though we can't do them perfectly, that is no reason to not do them at all. Reading the Bible begrudgingly is infinitely better than not reading the Bible at all!

I say all this in the attempt to explain why deeds matter, why there is a disconnect between the internal and external, and why it is sometimes necessary to talk ourselves into acts of righteousness. Now I want to narrow our focus by arguing that when Jesus commands us to love our neighbor, when he commands us to care for the "least of these," he is thereby commanding us to love and care for abortion-vulnerable children. The two passages that will drive this argument are Luke 10:25-37 and Matthew 25:31-46. The story of the Good Samaritan has had an unparalleled influence on my life—completely redirecting my vocational course, and the judgment of the sheep and the goats has become foundational to the way I understand Abort73's ministry. I am fairly convinced that there is no group of human beings more qualified to wear the "least of these" label than abortion-vulnerable children. Thematically, this is where the title of the book comes from. The call to love abortion-vulnerable children is a call to *Love the Least*.

For the first ten years of my Christian life, I was internally "pro-life," but externally "pro-choice." I believed abortion was wrong, I voted like abortion was wrong, but I lived as if it were no big deal. At the heart of my indifference was the idea that combating abortion is not a kingdom priority. *Abortion is a political issue... It's not my calling... Why should I waste my time trying to moralize unbelievers?* All of these excuses came crashing down on a Saturday morning in Nashville, when the story of the Good Samaritan was opened to me in a new light. Gregg Cunningham, the executive director for The Center for Bio-Ethical Reform, was in town for a one-day seminar. My mom knew Gregg and wanted me to meet him. The trip I had scheduled for the weekend fell through. The tiny Baptist church hosting the event was a few blocks from my apartment. So I went. In fact, I was almost the only one who went, but the sparseness of that gathering has been a frequent source of encouragement ever since. Gregg could have packed it in and not bothered with such a small crowd. But he didn't. And here I am. Central to his presentation was the story of the Good Samaritan—a story originally prompted by an extremely significant question: "what shall I do to inherit eternal life?"[8] When a lawyer asks this of Christ, Jesus asks him what is written in the Law. When the lawyer asks who his neighbor is, Jesus tells him the story of the Good Samaritan:

> A man was going down from Jerusalem to Jericho, and he fell among robbers, who stripped him and beat him and departed, leaving him half dead. Now by chance a priest was going down that road, and when

8   Luke 10:25

he saw him he passed by on the other side. So
likewise a Levite, when he came to the place
and saw him, passed by on the other side.
But a Samaritan, as he journeyed, came to
where he was, and when he saw him, he had
compassion. He went to him and bound up
his wounds, pouring on oil and wine. Then
he set him on his own animal and brought
him to an inn and took care of him. And the
next day he took out two denarii and gave
them to the innkeeper, saying, 'Take care of
him, and whatever more you spend, I will
repay you when I come back.' Which of these
three, do you think, proved to be a neighbor
to the man who fell among the robbers?" He
said, "The one who showed him mercy." And
Jesus said to him, "You go, and do likewise."[9]

Who is my neighbor? The nameless, unconscious, socially-
despised stranger on the brink of death. What does it mean to
love him? To physically intervene on his behalf, even if it cost
time, money, safety and prestige. Jesus builds his narrative on
"neighbors" so different, so detached, so disconnected, that
it becomes impossible to classify *anyone* as a non-neighbor.
And though it is a relatively extreme example, it illustrates
how far a genuine love for your neighbor is willing to go.
When we understand the story of the Good Samaritan, not
as an extraordinary act of kindness, but as an application of

---

9   Luke 10:30-37

normal, neighborly love in extraordinary circumstances, we're on the right track. But it still won't hit us like it should if we demonize the priest and Levite. When you view them as self-absorbed villains, it's much easier to escape conviction. When you see them as normal, busy, distracted people, the story hits much closer to home.

Jesus doesn't tell us what the priest and Levite were thinking, but it's unlikely that these spiritual icons were so hard hearted that they could look on a beaten countryman without feeling compassion. Nor is it hard to imagine the excuses that probably went through their heads. *I'm on my way to the Synagogue… I can't become ceremonially unclean… Mercy ministries aren't my calling… I'm not a doctor… Someone else will help… I might be attacked and robbed myself… He's probably dead already… I'll pray for him as I go.* Having used variants of these same excuses, I'm well aware how reasonable they sound in the moment. But Jesus makes it clear that feeling compassion and showing compassion are entirely different things. It doesn't matter what they *felt*, it matters what they *did*. Since they did nothing, they stand condemned.

At some point in his talk, Gregg asserted that most Christians are responding to abortion in the same way the priest and Levite responded to the beaten man in the street. They feel bad but pass the victims by. His assessment was certainly true of me. Like so many others, I thought mental opposition to abortion was enough. As long as I knew it was wrong and didn't endorse abortion myself, that was all I was accountable for. But what is the underlying warning in this passage? *It's not what we feel; it's what we do.* We can act without love,[10] but we cannot love without acting. Loving your neighbor is not a special calling; it's a response to those in need around you. And it's worth noting that the hero in this story was not wandering around looking for someone to help. He was on his way somewhere else, but he stopped to help a neighbor in need.

How does this story connect to abortion? The parallels are many. Just like the man left for dead in the street, children threatened by abortion are utterly helpless. If someone doesn't intervene, they will die. They have no capacity to communicate or ask for help. They are socially-marginalized strangers in a culture programmed not to care about them. And just like the people passing by on the Jericho road, we may be innocent of the crime, but Jesus still expects us to intervene. The violence of abortion is not as visible as a man lying beaten in the street, but it surrounds us every day. In the story of the Good Samaritan, Christ teaches us the significance of the insignificant. Even a nameless stranger on the brink of death is worth our time, labor, and love.

In some ways, the account of the sheep and the goats is an extension of the Good Samaritan. Jesus never uses the words "love" or "neighbor," but the lesson is much the same— with two additions. In this account, Jesus inserts himself into the equation and describes what happens to those who fail to serve those in need. In the prologue, Jesus declares that when he returns in glory, he will gather all the nations before his throne and separate them as a shepherd separates the sheep from the goats. This is the fate of the goats:

---

10 I Corinthians 13:3

> Then he will say to those on his left, "Depart from me, you cursed, into the eternal fire prepared for the devil and his angels. For I was hungry and you gave me no food, I was thirsty and you gave me no drink, I was a stranger and you did not welcome me, naked and you did not clothe me, sick and in prison and you did not visit me." Then they also will answer, saying, "Lord, when did we see you hungry or thirsty or a stranger or naked or sick or in prison, and did not minister to you?" Then he will answer them, saying, "Truly, I say to you, as you did not do it to one of the least of these, you did not do it to me." And these will go away into eternal punishment, but the righteous into eternal life.[11]

In making the case that abortion-vulnerable children may be fairly classified among the "least of these," I must start by acknowledging an interpretive concern some will take with this application. Though it's fairly common to hear the "least of these" tag applied to a broad range of people, the immediate context may be narrower—perhaps only referencing tribulation saints. I address this view in Appendix C. Please read it if you feel I'm distorting the text. Now consider the specific people that are listed in this passage. If you compare Christ's words to the sheep in verses 34-40, you'll notice that

---

11 Matthew 25:41-46

he includes the same, categorical list of people both times. Those described as the "least of these" in verses 40 and 45 are described as the hungry, the thirsty, the strangers, the naked, the sick, and the imprisoned in verses 35-36 and 42-43. Strictly speaking, abortion-vulnerable children satisfy one or two of these conditions and neither is contextually applicable. To understand this passage's application to abortion, we must take a deeper look at the categories of need represented in these six types.

The hungry, thirsty, sick, and naked can be fairly lumped together because of what will happen to them if their needs remain unmet. In each case if their condition persists, they will die. A body may survive for a month or two without food, but no more. Without water, it would be hard to last a week. In many climates, a man without clothes will die of exposure; in any climate, a naked man's prospects for survival are not good. A sick person may survive for a time, but the ultimate end of sickness is always death. It is not a lack of food, drink, clothes, or medicine that is the issue. The threat of death is the issue. Hunger, thirst, sickness, and exposure are just different paths to the same destination—and so is abortion. But instead of being an unintended byproduct, death is the *intended* result of abortion, and it comes a lot more quickly and violently.

If pending death binds four of the groups together, what is at stake for the stranger and prisoner? In some instances, particularly in the first century, strangers and prisoners faced the same threats as those we've already looked at. Prisoners were under fed, under clothed, and vulnerable to sickness and disease. Strangers, without the widespread availability of hotels, restaurants, and grocery stores, faced their own set of vulnerabilities. But more than their lack of resources, the stranger and prisoner are bound by isolation and helplessness. They are alone in the world. The stranger has no friends; the prisoner has no access to friends. Even if their physical lives are not immediately threatened, their well-being is—a condition made more desperate by their inability to help themselves. A prisoner without food is worse off than a free man without food. The free man can search for something to eat. He can work or gather or beg. A prisoner can't. Likewise, a stranger without food is worse off than a local without food. The local knows where to go. He has friends or family who can help. The stranger doesn't. He is without an advocate, and he may not even speak the language. Like both the prisoner and the stranger, abortion-vulnerable children are incapable of providing for their needs. Like the prisoner, they are hidden away; the world goes on around them, unaware of their existence and unaware that their lives are threatened. Like the stranger, abortion vulnerable children have no friends; like the stranger in a foreign land, abortion vulnerable children cannot communicate. They may have the bodily support of their mothers, but those mothers are contemplating their violent termination.

When you understand what is at stake for those Jesus describes as the "least of these," it becomes easier to see the connection to abortion-vulnerable children. They are threatened by the same thing. But the case for including them among the "least of these" doesn't end here. As I touched on in relation to the stranger and prisoner, it is the utter helplessness of abortion-vulnerable children that makes their plight so much more desperate. In the broader category of hungry people, there is a significant difference between the prospects of a grown man and an infant child. One has the capacity to look for food; the other does not. One has the capacity to feed himself; the other does not. If we're talking degrees of helplessness, the plight of abortion-vulnerable children is more akin to that of a starving, blind, mute paraplegic, hidden away in a dark alleyway than it is to the average beggar on the street. They can't be heard. They can't be seen. And even when someone becomes aware of them, there is no easy or obvious way to help.

Finally, in the relative affluence of America, lots of people in the situations Jesus describes bear some personal culpability for their condition. This is not always the case, but foolish, sinful choices have reduced the fortunes and health of untold millions. Jesus doesn't address this distinction in Matthew 25. He doesn't say to only feed and clothe those whose distress is *not* their own fault. He simply says to feed the hungry and clothe the naked. We are to have compassion on the wise and foolish alike. But in the grand scheme of things, who has a stronger claim to our benevolence—the one who has squandered his life away in loose living or the one who bears no guilt for what is threatening him? Doesn't a prisoner's condition become far more pitiable if he was wrongfully accused? Children in the womb have inherited a sin nature from Adam, but it has yet to manifest itself in a single, sinful choice. Union to Adam makes them guilty by association, but on the personal level, they have never sinned. For all the men and women who have died unjustly, they still deserved to die. Every sinner deserves to die. But for the child whose life ends in abortion, we can truly say that their death was not deserved.

For all these reasons, the real and imminent threat of death, the complete and utter inability to help themselves, the impossibility of communication, the hidden nature of their plight, the legal protection given to their assailants, the extremely narrow opportunities for intervention (not to mention the social cost of advocating on their behalf), I say again that there is no other group in the world more qualified to wear the "least of these" label than abortion-vulnerable children. At this point, perhaps you would like to remind me that there are an estimated 160 million orphans in the world today—orphans who are already born, who are suffering pain and neglect and malnutrition every day. How can I compare the plight of developing embryos and fetuses to theirs? If that's going through your mind right now, I would say first, my intention is not to get us to turn a blind eye to the downtrodden and oppressed who have already been born. My intention is to get us to open our eyes to the downtrodden and oppressed who haven't. Second, the argument I've just recounted, which is so commonly used to demonstrate why children in the womb are less significant than children outside the womb, is further evidence for why we can fairly classify abortion-vulnerable children among the "least of these." They are so marginalized that their very insignificance has become the primary rationale for their abuse *and* for the relative indifference to their abuse.

When Jesus stands before the nations and separates them as a shepherd separates the sheep from the goats, he will count service to the least as service to himself. Whatever you did for the least of these, you did for me. Whatever you did for the insignificant and marginalized, you did for me. Jesus is willing to personally identify with the hungry, the thirsty, and the naked. Would it be beneath him to identify with an abortion-vulnerable embryo or fetus? Have we forgotten that Jesus was an embryo? Have we forgotten that he was a fetus, conceived out of wedlock to a teenaged mom? Or that Herod was so fearful that Jesus might grow up to get in his way that he tried to have him aborted—after birth? The God of the universe humbled himself not just to become a man, but to become a child, an infant, a fetus, and an embryo! To those on his left, to those cursed with eternal fire, Jesus says, "I was hungry and you gave me no food, I was thirsty and you gave me no drink, I was a stranger and you did not welcome me, naked and you did not clothe me, sick and in prison and you did not visit me."12 Is it really such of a stretch to imagine him also saying, *I was in the womb and you gave me no care, I was threatened by abortion and you did not intervene, I was an embryo and you said I didn't matter, a fetus and you said there were more important things to do?*

The measuring stick of Christian love is not what we do for our friends. It's not what we do for the healthy and put together. It's what we do for the "least of these." Heaven and

---

12 Matthew 25:42-43

hell are on the line in our treatment of them—not because we need to earn God's favor, but because our treatment of them shows whether or not we've received God's favor. When we ignore the least of these, we show that our faith is flawed. At best, it is an unhealthy faith. At worst, it is a dead faith. At the end of the day, the battle to obey is nothing less than the battle to believe. This is the fight of faith. When you violate one of God's prohibitions, it is because you believe that the reward of sin will be greater than the reward of righteousness. This is true for the sins of commission *and* the sins of omission. We would do well to feel the weight of Christ's warning to the goats. Proverbs 16:6 says that the man who fears the Lord turns away from evil. The passages we looked at in Matthew and Luke teach us that it is evil to neglect the needs of our neighbors—including our neighbors in the womb. Put these two realities together and the conclusion is obvious. Those who fear the Lord cannot, will not, fail to love the least (a lot).

Chapter Five

LOVING CHRIST THROUGH LOVING ABORTION-VULNERABLE CHILDREN

EVANGELISM HAS ALWAYS TERRIFIED ME, but over the years, God has placed me in numerous, programmatic situations where it simply could not be avoided. As a freshman in high school, our discipleship group regularly spent Sunday afternoons at the Panorama City Mall—not to shop, but to share Jesus with anyone we could find milling around. The goal at the outset was to place a staff member in every group, but there weren't enough leaders to go around—forcing me to partner with a fellow student. Much to my chagrin, we then became the students who didn't need staff assistance. We continued these outings for the next couple years until increasing language barriers and more vigilant mall security made our efforts less manageable.

I spent the summer before my senior year of high school in an evangelism training program at church. There were a couple high school students and a couple hundred college students. Each week, we journeyed to the Santa Monica pier or LAX to proclaim the message of salvation through Jesus Christ. To this day, my clearest sense of the reality of

I Corinthians 1:18—*the message of the cross is foolishness to those who are perishing*—goes back to the sands of Santa Monica. As I stood there, a 17-year-old witnessing to a well-reasoned man twice my age, I couldn't shake the feeling that I was speaking absolute nonsense. I never doubted what I was proclaiming, but I could appreciate how utterly ridiculous it must sound to him.

In college, I was involved with Campus Crusade for Christ, so Friday afternoons were spent in the student union with a handful of Four Spiritual Laws tracts. After college, I was introduced to the street preaching ministry of Ray Comfort on a visit to the 3rd Street Promenade. Though I never did any preaching myself, we went back often to evangelize on the edges. More recently, my time on high school staff at Calvary Bible Church included a number of witnessing outings to downtown Burbank—where I had to set a good example for the students!

As a student, I always had the idea that evangelism would be easier when I was older. Now, that I'm older, I can't shake the feeling that it was easier when I was a student. In other words, evangelism is never easy, at least not for me. It always entails a level of mental exertion to get over that hump of awkwardness and fear. But what do I really have to fear? Over the course of my life, I have spoken with hundreds of strangers about Christ, and not one time has my life been threatened. All things considered, my evangelistic efforts have yielded very little persecution or contempt. I'm not complaining about that, but in light of Christ's frequent warnings, doesn't that strike you as odd? Consider the words of Jesus:

> You will be hated by all for my name's sake.[1]

> If the world hates you, know that it has hated me before it hated you... If they persecuted me, they will also persecute you.[2]

You will be hated by all for my name's sake. The disciples certainly found this to be true. They were beaten and killed for proclaiming the deity of Christ. Why haven't I been hated for proclaiming the same thing? Some suggest that the reason most American Christians don't experience any hatred for the sake of Christ is because most American Christians don't evangelize. That may be true, but as an American Christian who has evangelized, I was still coming up empty in the hatred department. I've met with lots of annoyance, but very little anger. If evangelism is the highest calling of the Christian life, why have I never been hated for doing it? After all, what could be more offensive than telling people that without Christ, they're headed for eternal destruction? On January 11, 1999, I found out. So far as I can tell, it was the first time I had ever been hated for my faith, and it had nothing to do with evangelism. It had to do with the Genocide Awareness Project—a traveling, photo-mural exhibit that compares abortion to modern and historic forms of genocide. By the end of my first day at the University of Florida, I had

---

1   Matthew 10:22
2   John 15:18-20a

learned a valuable lesson. In America today, the cost of being a public witness against abortion is much higher than the cost of telling people that Jesus died for their sins. Chalk it up to universalism, tolerance, or familiarity, but a general expression of faith in Jesus doesn't rile a lot of feathers.

Over the course of that year, I would travel to university campuses across Florida, Ohio, Oregon, and Washington—including a visit to Washington State University, where I had been a student less than two years before. On almost the same spot where I had often met with indifference as an evangelist, I met with hatred as an activist. Tame and tolerant dismissals gave way to passionate and heated engagement. Post-modern college students are fairly adept at cordially dismissing evangelism, but things change when the topic turns to abortion. Their apathetic agnosticism suddenly vanishes and the truth becomes very knowable. Somewhere between my first campus tour in the spring and my second tour in the fall, I read Francis Schaeffer's, *The God Who is There*. Early on, he includes the following quote from Martin Luther:

> If we profess with the loudest voice and clearest exposition every portion of the truth of God except precisely that little point which the world and the devil are at the moment attacking, I am not confessing Christ, however boldly I may be professing Christ. Where the battle rages, there the loyalty of the soldier is proved, and to be steady on

all the battlefield besides, is mere flight and
disgrace if he flinches at that point.[3]

*Where the battle rages... that little point which the world and
the devil are at the moment attacking... there the loyalty of the
soldier is proved.* Martin Luther did not make this statement
with abortion in mind, but when I first read it, that's exactly
where my mind went. After five weeks at some of the largest
state schools in Florida, facing persecution and contempt the
likes of which I'd never experienced before, where else could
my mind go? It would be 12 years before I heard anyone else
connect Luther's quote to abortion. In a sermon delivered
on July 3, 2011, David Platt read these same words as an
indictment against his own indifference, commenting that "if
[we] sit idly by while millions of children... are dismembered
and destroyed, and we do nothing... that is sin."[4]

The reason I had never publicly connected Luther's
quote to abortion is because abortion is *my* issue, so to speak,
and pride is an ugly thing—whether you're talking about
yourself or your calling. Framing this statement in the context
of abortion is to essentially infer: *It doesn't matter what you say
or do about anything else. If you are not being a witness against
abortion, your faithfulness in other matters is a cowardly retreat.*
As a paid, anti-abortion advocate, that could sound like a
fairly self-serving assertion—which is why I've never made

3   Schaeffer, Francis. *Trilogy: The Three Essential Books in One Volume.*
     (Wheaton: Crossway, 1990) 11.

4   Platt, David. "The Children Yet Unborn." The Church at Brook Hills. 3 July
     2011. <http://www.radical.net/media/series/view/516/the-children-yet-
     unborn>.

it. But David Platt *did* make it, at least in measure, and that is a remarkable thing. Abortion is not his pet issue, not by a long shot. He has poured himself out on many fronts, but not this one, not yet—which is why he can speak of it in such forceful terms, without fear of sounding self-righteous. In many ways, those whose vocations are less tied to abortion have less need to mince their words when asserting the primacy of combating it. When I say passivity to abortion is a sin, I may just be lining my pockets. When David Platt says the same thing, it's much harder to argue with.

Not only did my post-college, campus experience teach me that being a witness against abortion brings a lot more hostility than general evangelism, I also learned that most campus ministries wanted NOTHING to do with this issue. One way or another, they told us that their involvement would do too much damage to their reputation and too much damage to the gospel. More recently, a friend and advocate sought to create a partnership between Abort73 and the network of churches he's involved with. After gaining an audience with the director, this was their response (through my friend):

> You have the full support of [their church network] but they avoid political-type affiliations… the general idea is that if they are going to polarize people, they want it to be the gospel that does so and not other issues… Rest assured you are supported and prayed for.

In both instances, the campus ministry refusals to publicly identify with the Genocide Awareness Project and the church network's refusal to publicly identify with Abort73, it was an appeal to the gospel that anchored their rationale for not getting involved—the same conviction that fueled my own inaction for so many years. And even when I reversed field and joined The Center for Bio-Ethical Reform, it wasn't because I saw it as gospel work. I saw it as important work, and that was enough for me. In retrospect, I may have been selling the gospel short. Consider the remarks of longtime, civil rights activist John M. Perkins:

> I do not understand why so many evangelicals find a sense of commitment to civil rights and to Jesus Christ an "either-or" proposition. One of the greatest tragedies of the civil rights movement is that evangelicals surrendered their leadership in the movement by default to those with either a bankrupt theology or no theology at all, simply because the vast majority of Bible-believing Christians ignored a great and crucial opportunity in history for genuine ethical action. The evangelical church—whose basic theology is the same as mine—had not gone on to preach whole gospel.[5]

Perkins equates the evangelical church's refusal to combat racism, not with a failure to move beyond the gospel, but

---

5   Perkins, John. *Let Justice Roll Down*. (Ventura: Regal, 1976) 99.

with a failure to preach the whole gospel. If evangelicals would have preached the whole gospel, he contends, they would have preached against the manifold injustices of racial bigotry. And that brings us to the question at the heart of this chapter. What is the gospel? Have you ever stopped to wrestle with that? It's such a ubiquitous term in Christian circles that we rarely stop to define it. The literal meaning, "good news," is commonly known, but what *is* the good news? In some ways, the answer seems obvious. *Jesus died to save sinners!*[6] But what about the fact that the disciples proclaimed the gospel *before* Jesus died,[7] and before they knew he would die? Three times in the book of Mark, Jesus foretold his death and resurrection,[8] but the disciples completely missed it. On this point, the Pharisees were far more astute than the twelve, posting a guard at Christ's tomb to prevent a feigned resurrection.[9] Meanwhile, the disciples hid in despair—and were perfectly dumbstruck by the empty tomb. Clearly, the gospel they were preaching bore no mention of Jesus' death and resurrection— which must mean that gospel proclamation entails more than giving an account of Calvary.

If you want an interesting exercise, start at the beginning of Matthew and note every instance of the word "gospel" in the four gospels. Pretend you have no prior knowledge of the term and must decipher its meaning from the text alone. It's a little maddening. The authors seem to take it for granted that the reader already knows what "gospel" means, so they

---

6   I Corinthians 15:1-3

7   Luke 9:6

8   Mark 8:31, 9:31, 10:34

9   Matthew 27:62-64

don't bother explaining it—despite the fact that it never appears in the Old Testament. In most English Bibles, its first use is in Matthew 4:23: "[Jesus] went throughout all Galilee, teaching in their synagogues and proclaiming the gospel of the kingdom and healing every disease and every affliction among the people." There's nothing in the context of the verse to define the term—a pattern that extends through much of Scripture.

In English, the word gospel has an explicitly religious origin. It is a phrase for phrase rendering of the Greek word, *euangelion* (eu- "good", -angelion "message"), into Old English, (gōd-spell, ie "good news"). Strangely, at least to my limited sensibility, the phrase-for-phrase translation has not been carried over to modern English. Instead of going from gōd-spell to "good news," the more literal translations go from gōd-spell to "gospel." And while "gospel" has now become part of the English vernacular, that doesn't make it any easier to define. By all accounts, nobody used "good message" in such a singular way before the arrival of Christ, and he did so from the very outset of his public ministry. His first recorded words in Mark read, "The time is fulfilled, and the kingdom of God is at hand; repent and believe in the gospel."[10] Matthew offers a shorter rendering of the same basic message.[11] The biggest clue to Christ's appropriation of "good news" comes during his first public statement in Luke. Standing up to teach in the synagogue, Jesus unrolls the scroll of Isaiah and reads from what is now chapter 61:

---

10 Mark 1:15
11 Matthew 4:17

> The Spirit of the Lord is upon me, because
> he has anointed me to proclaim good news
> to the poor. He has sent me to proclaim
> liberty to the captives and recovering of sight
> to the blind, to set at liberty those who are
> oppressed, to proclaim the year of the Lord's
> favor.[12]

Jesus then hands the scroll back to the attendant and formally announces the commencement of his Messianic ministry: "Today this Scripture has been fulfilled in your hearing." If you read this passage in the NAS or King James, you'll find that it renders "good news" as "gospel," but if you read the original prophesy from Isaiah, the translation is different. The NAS reads "good news;" the King James reads "good tidings." Perplexing, isn't it? What seems to have happened is that Jesus took the first item from Isaiah's list of messianic offices (proclaiming good news to the poor) and makes it an umbrella term to signify the whole of God's redemptive plan. He didn't redefine the term, but he certainly gave it a significance beyond what it had known before—which may be why more English Bibles don't translate gospel as "good news."

Though I'm tempted to chase this rabbit trail further, the central question for us is not why Jesus singled out "gospel" in the first place or why it's translated the way it is, but what he meant by it. What is the gospel we're called to believe? What is the gospel we're called to proclaim? When

---

12 Luke 4:18-19

Jesus stands before his disciples in Mark 16:15 and says, "Go into all the world and proclaim the gospel to the whole creation," what is the precise message he wants us to deliver? Mark 16:16 provides more context: "Whoever believes and is baptized will be saved, but whoever does not believe will be condemned." Reading that, it's understandable why so many take a narrowly evangelistic view of the Great Commission and distance themselves from ministries with less soul-saving objectives. I ran up against such thinking a couple years ago at an Abort73 outreach event. The large church where it was held allowed us the unprecedented blessing of almost taking over their evening service. As we set up our tables in the lobby, the senior pastor insisted that we move them to a more prominent location so that everyone would see them. But right before we went onstage, he said to me, "Just so I know we're on the same page, you'd say the primary goal of Abort73 is to tell people about Jesus, right?" For a moment I thought he was being facetious. How could anyone with as much familiarity with Abort73 come to that conclusion? When it became apparent he wasn't joking, I responded that evangelism was not our primary goal. Suddenly a minor crisis was under way. "What does it matter if you convince a woman not to have an abortion, if she doesn't get saved?" he asked. "It's like fumbling the ball at the goal line." "It matters for the baby," I answered. My memory fails me a bit here, but he responded with something like: "Not if the baby grows up to reject Christ." As it turned out, we weren't as far apart as it initially seemed. Like Paul and James, we had some semantic obstacles to work through, but once I assured him that I wasn't trying to jettison the cross or preach a social gospel, we were good to go. Though this particular evening turned out well, there are still plenty of evangelicals who seem to view any service short of salvation as meaningless.

At this point, it would be helpful to consider Matthew's rendering of the Great Commission. To truly understand the more abbreviated directive found in Mark (which may have been added by an entirely different author), we still must unpack what it means to "proclaim the gospel." Matthew's account helps shed some light. It reads, "Go therefore and make disciples of all nations, baptizing them in the name of the Father and of the Son and of the Holy Spirit, teaching them to observe all that I have commanded you."[13] Putting the two accounts side by side, we can say that proclaiming the gospel aims at making disciples, seeing them baptized, and teaching them to observe everything that Jesus commanded. If the emphasis in Mark is to make converts, the emphasis in Matthew is to make disciples. But aren't converts and disciples the same thing? Yes, unless you view conversion as merely getting people to sign off on a minimally invasive statement of faith (instead of seeing them transformed into the likeness of Christ). If your aim is to get people to say a prayer and sign a card, then of course it makes sense to avoid contentious sin issues like abortion. But are low-grade commitments really what Christ is after?

There are two recorded instances of Jesus being asked the quintessential gospel question: *what must I do to be saved?* Nothing in either response hints at easy-believe-ism. Both

---

13 Matthew 28:19-20

answers are variants of "obey the commandments." Since neither the rich young ruler in Matthew 19 nor the lawyer in Luke 10 can bring himself to admit his guilt, Jesus never even gets to repentance and belief. He lets them walk away. And the first commandment Jesus listed when responding to the rich young ruler was, "Do not murder." That's something to consider if you count the public condemnation of abortion (an application of "do not murder") a hindrance to the gospel. Over and over again, Jesus says things that make it hard for people to believe. His most articulate, theological explanation of substitutionary atonement is rooted in cannibalistic imagery.[14] It left his audience so outraged that many disciples walked away. According to Jesus, it's not only hard for people to believe, it's *impossible*—but for God.[15] So we needn't try and make the gospel more palatable than Jesus did. The goal of evangelism is not mental assent to a bare minimum of beliefs. The goal is total transformation—the full embrace of all that Christ commanded.

While some Christians jettison the abortion issue for fear of giving offense, others do so because they fear it's a distraction. They're not trying to soft-sell the message; they're simply trying to stay on task. Their theme verse is I Corinthians 2:2: "I have determined to know nothing among you but Christ crucified." For many years, this is the verse I would have used to justify my own non-engagement on the abortion front. And though I've now reversed field, this verse doesn't go away. If I can't combat abortion under the

14 John 6:22-66
15 Matthew 19:26

umbrella of knowing nothing but Christ, I've got a problem. But before we go any further, we should consider what Paul actually meant. Is he saying that the crucifixion is the only thing he ever talked about *or* that the crucifixion anchors and motivates everything he did? Without question, it is the latter. When he sought out the apostles to ensure the gospel he was preaching was not in vain,[16] Peter, James, and John gladly extended him the right hand of fellowship, but reminded him to not forget the poor. And Paul's concern for the poor clearly went beyond preaching, as evidenced by his ongoing monetary relief efforts.[17] Even more significant, perhaps, is the fact that when Paul found out that Peter and Barnabas were segregating themselves from Gentiles, he declared that "their conduct was not in step with the truth of the gospel."[18] I can almost hear John Perkins saying, "Amen!" It's impossible to teach all that Christ has commanded if you only teach about the crucifixion.

Now, I'll take it one step further. Not only is it possible to combat abortion without compromising Paul's directive to know "nothing but Christ," I would argue that it is necessary. I don't mean devotion to Christ is a necessary component of combating abortion. I mean combating abortion is a necessary component of devotion to Christ. Why? Because the failure to love abortion-vulnerable children is the failure to love Jesus Christ. I say that in light of what Jesus says in Matthew 18:5 and Matthew 25:40. But before we look at

---

16 Galatians 2:2
17 Romans 15:25-26, I Corinthians 16:1-3, 2 Corinthians 8-9.
18 Galatians 2:14

these texts, consider Jesus' remarkable promise to the 12 disciples in Matthew 10:40: "Whoever receives you receives me, and whoever receives me receives him who sent me." Jesus commissioned the apostles with the astounding privilege of being his bodily representatives. Whoever received them received him and in turn, the Father who sent him. Any act of kindness, service, or love done for the disciples was counted as direct service to Jesus the Christ. Even a cup of cold water did not go unrewarded.

The apostles no longer walk the earth today, but Jesus gave this same representative office to two other groups of people. Both of them remain en masse. The first group is young, marginalized children. The second group is those deemed the "least of these." We've already read Christ's rebuke of the goats for ignoring the least among them. Now let's read his rebuke to the disciples for ignoring the children among them:

> At that time the disciples came to Jesus, saying, "Who is the greatest in the kingdom of heaven?" And calling to him a child, he put him in the midst of them and said, "Truly, I say to you, unless you turn and become like children, you will never enter the kingdom of heaven. Whoever humbles himself like this child is the greatest in the kingdom of heaven. "Whoever receives one such child in my name receives me, but whoever causes one of these little ones who believe in me to

> sin, it would be better for him to have a great
> millstone fastened around his neck and to be
> drowned in the depth of the sea."[19]

Whoever receives a child, receives Jesus. When the disciples try and scurry away the children coming to Jesus in the next chapter, he rebukes them. "Let the little children come to me and do not hinder them, for to such belongs the kingdom of heaven."[20] Jesus publicly identifies himself with both young children and the hungry, thirsty, naked, sick, imprisoned, and estranged. If you think about it, it is not an arbitrary connection. Jesus *was* a marginalized young child, conceived out of wedlock and born in a barn. Not only did he come into the world as a child, but he became *like* a child in his humble devotion to the father.[21] And of course Jesus knew hunger and thirst. He knew what it was to be without a home, to be a stranger among hostile enemies, sick, imprisoned, and naked. He shared these afflictions as well. But here is where it gets most compelling. If you take the two groups that Jesus aligns himself with and combine them together, you get abortion-vulnerable children. They are marginalized young children; they are helpless and oppressed. To receive them and care for them is to receive and care for Jesus. Likewise, to distance ourselves from the active condemnation of abortion, whether intentionally or not, is to distance ourselves from Christ.

In bringing this chapter to a close, let's consider again the warning Jesus makes to those who follow him. "You

19 Matthew 18:1-6
20 Matthew 19:14
21 John 5:19

will be hated by all for my name's sake… If they persecuted me, they will also persecute you."[22] Did the world persecute Jesus? Yes. They persecuted him to death, which leaves only one option. If we're not being persecuted, we're not following Jesus. But before we jump to a wrong conclusion, it would be good to note two things. First, Jesus doesn't command us to seek persecution. He simply tells us that persecution will come to those who follow him. If we miss this distinction, we risk making an idol out of contempt. You can be persecuted without being godly; you just can't be godly without being persecuted.

It is also important to note that much of what Jesus did earned him praise and adoration. The hatred he encountered was sporadic and isolated. Being always hated by everyone is just as dangerous as never being hated by anyone. Jesus says to let our light shine before men so they will see and glorify the Father. He expects people to be attracted to our life. That doesn't happen if we're only giving offense. Jesus and the apostles performed miracles to gain credibility through practical acts of compassion and to demonstrate that Jesus has authority to forgive sins.[23] They weren't simply to demonstrate supernatural power. In most instances, the recipients were so grateful they would have believed anything Jesus asked of them. So long as Jesus was healing the sick and feeding the hungry, he was extremely popular. You could rightly call him the most popular man in the world. So how could he have been hated enough to be nailed to a tree?

---

22 Matthew 10:22, 24:9, Mark 13:13, Luke 21:17, John 15:20
23 Matthew 9:6

In large measure, Jesus was loved for what he did and hated for what he said. That's an oversimplification, but it provides a helpful framework. And even when Jesus was hated for something he did (like healing on the Sabbath or clearing the temple), it was his explanation that elicited the most anger: *The Son of Man is Lord of the Sabbath. My house shall be called a house of prayer, but you make it a den of robbers.* Almost everything Jesus did irked the religious rulers, and it always boiled down to a question of authority. They were willing to worship God so long as they could do it on their terms. It is much the same today.

The reason evangelism isn't more offensive to more Americans is because so many Americans have a warped understanding of the gospel. They're familiar with the notion that Jesus died on a cross to save sinners, but they don't grasp how perilous their condition actually is, or that devotion to Christ demands every corner of their life. And even if you get them to concede that they're a lying, cheating, murdering, adulterer, they're still not likely to take much offense. Why? Because they're largely inoculated to the message: it's a joke to them. They'll let you believe and proclaim anything you want, so long as that belief doesn't infringe upon the public square.

Ours is a lukewarm culture that refuses to be hot or cold—until you attack the god of the system—and abortion is one of those gods. If you want to be a more effective evangelist, be a more faithful witness against abortion. Francis Schaeffer writes that, "the Christian must resist the spirit of the world in the form it takes in his own generation.

If he does not do this, he is not resisting the spirit of the world at all."[24] For whatever reason abortion cuts through the haze of polite indifference and creates engagement that is hard to come by in any other context. If you read the "Abortion Regrets" section of the Abort73 website, you'll find pages of testimonies from women who have had an abortion, have realized what a dreadful thing they've done, and have been reduced to despair. They are ready for the good news because for the first time in their lives, they've felt the weight of the bad news. It is sorrow that leads to repentance.

Jesus was hated for exposing sin. The good news he proclaimed was delivered on the heels of very bad news: *Woe to you, scribes and Pharisees, hypocrites! For you shut the kingdom of heaven in people's faces... you travel across sea and land to make a single proselyte, and when he becomes a proselyte, you make him twice as much a child of hell as yourselves... you tithe mint and dill and cumin, and have neglected the weightier matters of the law: justice and mercy and faithfulness... You blind guides, straining out a gnat and swallowing a camel!... you clean the outside of the cup and the plate, but inside [you] are full of greed and self-indulgence... you are like whitewashed tombs... full of dead people's bones and all uncleanness... you are sons of those who murdered the prophets... You serpents, you brood of vipers, how are you to escape being sentenced to hell?*

Implicit in the warning that we will be hated by the world is the assumption that we will be exposing sin.[25] And

24 Schaeffer, Francis. *Trilogy: The Three Essential Books in One Volume.*
    (Wheaton: Crossway, 1990) 11.

25 Ephesians 5:11

there isn't a sin in the world more contentious and more deserving of public exposure than abortion. Whether you count opposition to abortion as gospel work or not, the fact remains that it presents a remarkable opportunity for evangelism. I do not say that evangelism is the main reason for combating abortion, but I had more quality opportunities to proclaim the death and resurrection of Jesus Christ during my first month with the Genocide Awareness Project than I did in ten years of evangelizing on the street. When the person you're sharing with is engaged and connected, the good news becomes less of a sales pitch and more of a solution. *The world is a mess. We're killing our children in droves. But the coming King is merciful. These are the terms of peace.* If you find that you're not experiencing any of the hatred Jesus promises to those who follow him, chances are you haven't been exposing the sin of abortion.

Chapter Six

WHY WE IGNORE ABORTION

THE MOST INFLUENTIAL SERMON I've heard about abortion was preached by John Piper on January 24, 1999. It came to me as all of John's sermons did at that time: on a white cassette tape. The message was titled, "Visiting Orphans in a World of AIDS and Abortion," and was built around James 1:27: "Religion that is pure and undefiled before God, the Father, is this: to visit orphans and widows in their affliction, and to keep oneself unstained from the world." At around the 8-minute mark, Piper makes an observation that I've borrowed countless times since. It's a fitting launch point for this chapter. Commenting on "pure and undefiled religion," he says there is a horse to ride, biblically, and notes how easy it is to fall off the saddle on one side or the other—and break your neck! Some are falling off on the "personal piety" side, and others are falling off on the "social justice" side. He articulates the division this way:

> There are a lot of Christians who like the second half (of James 1:27): *sexual purity, financial integrity, keep a clean thought life,*

> *Amen. And let's stay home and watch TV...*
> And there is another group of Christians
> who say, *Hit the streets. It's justice that counts;*
> *it's peace that counts... Get off your seat and be*
> *a Christian.* And live like the devil in your
> bedroom and in front of your computer.

On one side, you have those who almost exclusively equate
holiness with the faithful adherence to personal, spiritual
disciplines. In an effort to remain unstained from the world,
they're "strong" on personal holiness but weak on cultural
engagement. On the other side, you've got those who are
extremely active in ministering to the poor and oppressed
but are far too casual with Scripture's demands for personal
holiness. In reaching out to their world, they've become
almost indistinguishable from the world. At the heart of
Pastor John's sermon is the plea for Christians to be both/
and, not either/or. God's people should be marked by
personal holiness *and* public service, not one or the other.
True religion is keeping oneself unstained from the world *and*
visiting orphans and widows. What a tragedy then that we see
so much lopsided Christianity in the world—if we can even
call it Christianity. As Piper notes, something very serious is
at stake in the way James defines saving faith. Quoting from
the sermon again:

> You can't divide [personal piety from social
> engagement] if you want to be biblical and
> if you want to avoid James' censure that

> your religion is empty. There are a lot of
> things that motivate people [towards] one
> while neglecting the other... If you're only
> motivated in one direction, you need to
> check to see if this is coming from Christ. If
> it *isn't* coming from Christ, who's whole, it
> probably isn't coming from faith. And you
> may wonder if you're a Christian and *should*
> wonder if you're a Christian.

What's at stake is not necessarily the difference between
being a biblically balanced Christian or a biblically
unbalanced Christian. It may well be the difference between
being a Christian and being a *non*-Christian. In the flesh, it is
relatively easy to take up residence on one side of the saddle
or the other. It is only when we are led by the Spirit that we can
move beyond the commands that are more naturally suited
to our personality (or church tradition) and embrace those
that aren't. And were we to examine these dual demands at
any length, we'd quickly see that to fall off the saddle on either
side is to miss the mark on *both* sides. Think of it in terms of
the greatest commandment. You might say that the personal
piety crowd is falling off on the "Love God" side while the
social justice crowd is falling off on the "Love your neighbor"
side. Here's the problem with setting the equation up this way.
Loving God and loving your neighbor move you in the *same*
direction. These are not competing ends. If we're loving God
in a way that neglects our neighbor, we're not really loving
God. If we're loving our neighbor in a way that neglects

God, we're not really loving our neighbor. In other words, it would be foolhardy to look for solace in our displacement by saying, "at least I'm living a holy life," or, "at least I'm loving my neighbor." There is no personal holiness apart from loving our neighbor and there is no genuine love for neighbor apart from personal holiness.

For the bulk of the last century, most evangelical churches have been falling off on the personal piety side of the saddle—emphasizing personal holiness and evangelism, but neglecting the physical needs of the poor and oppressed. Thankfully, a re-centering is well under way so that social justice causes are no longer the exclusive domain of theologically liberal churches. Gary Haugen, president and CEO of International Justice Mission (IJM), has been at the forefront of this charge, and the preface to the tenth anniversary edition of his book, *Good News About Injustice*, speaks to this evangelical shift:

> The reason for writing *Good News About Injustice* was very simple: in 1999 there were very few articles about justice [and] no book-length treatment of the problem of injustice in the world, God's view of it, and the role of God's people in addressing it. This seemed an absurd state of affairs considering the magnitude of the problem [and] the massive portions of the Bible that address this problem.
>
> ...
>
> In 2009, however, we must acknowledge that a sea of change has taken place.

A transformation of stunning speed and breadth is altering the Christian community—a transformation that offers great hope for the body of Christ and the world. Discussions of biblical justice are bursting into the mainstream Christian dialogue, church leadership, and ministry.[1]

That's the good news about injustice. Here's the bad news: As Christians around the world have taken on the needs of the poor and oppressed, abortion-vulnerable children have largely been left by the wayside. At best, they're being neglected; at worst, they're being shunned. I've seen this in a number of ways. Some months ago, I was at a lecture on international adoption, and the Christian speaker began by listing some of the global threats facing children today. Among other things, that list included sex trafficking, slavery, HIV/Aids, homelessness, disability, and incarceration. It did not include abortion. Since abortion kills upwards of 50 million children a year, this struck me as a significant omission. I emailed him after the conference to see if abortion was intentionally left off the list. He quickly responded that it had been a simple oversight and agreed that abortion should have been listed.

A much more serious form of neglect came to my attention a few weeks later, after the Canadian government refused to include abortion funding in their G8 campaign to improve maternal and child health in developing nations.

---

1   Haugen, Gary. *Good News About Injustice, Updated 10th Anniversary Edition: A Witness of Courage in a Hurting World.* (Downer's Grove: IVP Books, 2009) 20-21.

Their stance was roundly criticized by a well-known Christian relief and advocacy organization. The public statement of condemnation was signed by their CEO and posted to their website. Included in that statement was the following:

> Instead of pushing forward in support of an initiative that could benefit millions, we're allowing the potential for hope and opportunity to be swallowed up by a political debate about abortion that is stifling the potential for progress... [I]f lack of agreement on one issue forces the G8 to delay a decision on this maternal and child health initiative, another 8.8 million children and over 300,000 mothers will die waiting. We cannot allow these lives to slip away while we take up a debate on abortion here in Canada.[2]

The press release reads like something I'd expect from Planned Parenthood or Action Canada, not from followers of Christ. As reported by *The Vancouver Sun*, the only part of the maternal, child, and health package that the Canadian government would *not* be funding was abortion. Everything else was included. Healthcare training, disease treatment and prevention, STD screening, immunizations, clean

---

2 "Time to Measure Success in Lives Saved, Not Political Points Scored: Development leaders Say." World Vision Canada. 27 Apr. 2010. < http://www.worldvision.ca/About-Us/Newsroom/press-releases/Pages/time-to-measure-success-in-lives-saved.aspx >.

water access, sanitation, and even birth control would all be funded. In other words, the claim put forth by this Christian organization that "another 8.8 million children and over 300,000 mothers will die" if the Canadian government will not pay for abortions in developing nations seems nothing more than a hysteric distortion. Do free abortions save children from "painful, preventable illnesses?" Is abortion the cure to "malaria, diarrhea, and pneumonia?"

This is a Christian organization, made up of men and women who are investing their vocational lives to combat global poverty and oppression, and yet they see abortion as a distraction—as something that gets in the way of more pressing needs. This is not a matter of simply forgetting about abortion-vulnerable children. It's a matter of considering their plight and concluding that they don't matter—which brings me back to the horse and saddle. The reason this widespread movement towards a more biblically balanced life has yet to provide much relief for those threatened by abortion is because prior to this shift, abortion was being neglected by people on *both* sides of the saddle. Abortion was never even on the horse. Those on the personal piety side don't want to be associated with political activism, and those on the social activism side don't want to be associated with conservative politics.

But here's where it really gets complicated. While abortion is largely overlooked on both sides of the metaphorical horse, there is a perception in the world that abortion and gay marriage are the only issues Christians care about. The disconnect first struck me when I posted a link to Bryan Kemper's book, *Social Justice Begins in the Womb*, to Abort73's Facebook page. Shortly after the post went up, someone commented back: "Unfortunately for your crowd, social justice usually ends after the womb as well." I can't say for certain who he has in mind when he says, "your crowd," but I suspect he's taking aim at those in the church. No matter how you frame the arguments, opposition to abortion is almost always perceived as religiously motivated. The first 35 pages of Abort73's *Case Against Abortion* are thoroughly "secular" in nature. They bear no mention of the Bible, yet we still hear frequent variations of the same basic message: *Stop forcing your religion on me!*

The claim that Christians only care about people *before* they're born is not a new one, but this was the first time I stopped to think about where this perception is coming from. How could anyone get the impression that Christians (who can be as indifferent to abortion as the rest of the world) are obsessed with the abortion issue? I've met plenty of Christians who are almost obsessed with *avoiding* the abortion issue. For more than ten years, I've worked to lovingly, graciously combat the church's general apathy towards abortion—to wake Christians up, not just to the plight of *born* orphans, but also to the plight of *unborn* orphans. Though I love my work, there are times when I dread telling fellow believers what I do. I grow weary of the patronizing smiles and blank stares. Some personalities are wired for conflict. Mine is not. I'm about as mild-mannered as they come, but my connection to the abortion issue makes me a pariah of sorts—both inside and outside the church. If Christians were obsessed with combating abortion, wouldn't our ministry be a lot more popular than it is?

As I thought about this dichotomy more, it didn't take long to formulate a hypothesis: *Political Obsession; Practical Neglect.* That's the title of a blog I posted on the subject. On a political level, it probably *is* fair to say that Christians are hyper-focused on the abortion issue. On a practical level, it is quite the opposite. The Barna Group published a study during the lead up to the 2008 presidential election that examined America's perception of "evangelical voters." Among non-Christians, 58% of those surveyed "felt that evangelical voters would focus primarily on homosexuality and abortion."[3] I'm actually surprised that number wasn't higher. It probably *should* have been higher. In a separate Barna study published earlier in the year, 94% of evangelicals identified abortion as a "major problem" facing the country.[4] That easily outdistanced the second most problematic issue, personal debt, which was classified as a major problem by 81% of evangelicals. Though only 40% of evangelical voters in the 2008 presidential election identified "moral concerns" as their primary voting focus,[5] there's no getting around the fact that when it comes to the ballot box, evangelicals feel strongly about abortion.

3   "How Americans View 'Evangelical Voters." The Barna Group, Ltd, 9 Sep. 2008 <http://www.barna.org/barna-update/article/14-media/24-how-americans-view-evangelical-voters>.

4   "Americans Describe Their Moral and Social Concerns, Including Abortion and Homosexuality." The Barna Group, Ltd, 21 Jan. 2008 <http://www.barna.org/barna-update/article/13-culture/50-americans-describe-their-moral-and-social-concerns-including-abortion-and-homosexuality>.

5   "How People of Faith Voted in the 2008 Presidential Race." The Barna Group, Ltd, 11 Nov. 2008 <http://www.barna.org/barna-update/article/13-culture/18-how-people-of-faith-voted-in-the-2008-presidential-race>.

And it's not just evangelicals. Sixty-seven percent of born-again Christians believe abortion is a major problem, as do 56% of Protestants and 52% of Catholics.[6]

Anyone who is skeptical of survey data (and we all should be) will look at the numbers above and immediately want to know one thing: How are these rather fuzzy and often overlapping labels (evangelical, born again, Protestant, etc.) being applied? What makes an evangelical an evangelical? In the Barna studies, respondents are classified as Christian if they choose one of the following church affiliations: Mainline denomination,[7] Non-Mainline denomination,[8] or Catholic.[9] But unlike most surveys, the Barna Group employs a fairly sophisticated, 9-question, theological survey to dig a little deeper. They don't simply accept the religious labels people give themselves. Someone can say they're "born again," but if they don't believe like someone who's been born again, Barna doesn't classify them as such. Interestingly, in the study following the 2008 presidential election, Barna found that 41% of their respondents identified themselves as evangelicals, but only 7% affirmed the necessary statements of faith to be classified as evangelicals.[10] Clearly there is a

6   Americans Describe Their Moral and Social Concerns, Including Abortion and Homosexuality." The Barna Group, Ltd, 21 Jan. 2008 <http://www. barna.org/barna-update/article/13-culture/50-americans-describe-their-moral-and-social-concerns-including-abortion-and-homosexuality>.

7   including Episcopal, Evangelical Lutheran Church of America, United Church of Christ, United Methodist, and Presbyterian Church in the USA

8   attendees of Protestant churches that do not meet the criteria for mainline

9   identify with a Catholic denomination including Roman Catholic

10 "How People of Faith Voted in the 2008 Presidential Race." The Barna Group, Ltd, 11 Nov. 2008 <http://www.barna.org/barna-update/article/13-culture/18-how-people-of-faith-voted-in-the-2008-presidential-race>.

disconnect between what many people think they believe and what they actually believe. In light of this reality, I suggest that we take the findings that 94% of evangelicals see abortion as a "major problem" with a grain of salt. Just as people have a tendency to overstate their religious devotion, evangelicals have a tendency to overstate their opposition to abortion—saying, in theory, that abortion is a major problem but living, in practice, as if it's no big deal. Since there are lots of self-identified evangelicals who don't care much about the Bible, should we be surprised to find lots of self-identified "pro-lifers" who don't care much about abortion? If Barna employed a 9-question survey to determine whether people who say they oppose abortion actually live like they oppose abortion, I'm guessing the numbers would be very different.

Nevertheless, because so many people outside the church see Christianity through the lens of Republican politics, and because so many Christians do remember abortion once election season rolls around, there are all sorts of misconceptions relating to the priorities of the church. When Massachusetts Democrat Barney Frank says, "[For Republicans], life begins at conception but ends at birth,"[11] he may not be specifically calling out the church, but in many minds, there is no distinction.

At this point, perhaps you're saying, "so what?" What does it matter if the world thinks Christians are more concerned with abortion than they actually are? Should we

---

11 Frank, Barney. Interview with Al Sharpton. *PoliticsNation*, 2 Feb. 2012.
   <http://www.msnbc.msn.com/id/46253770/ns/msnbc-politicsnation/t/
   politicsnation-thursday-february/>.

even care what the world thinks? And if abortion is one of the clearest expressions of evil in the physical realm, isn't this a misconception in the church's favor? Not exactly. The problem I have in mind is not that opposition to abortion is almost exclusively associated with Christianity. Opposition to abortion *should* be associated with Christianity. Christians should be at the forefront of defending the weak and fatherless. The real problem lies elsewhere, and it is threefold. Number one, opposition to abortion shouldn't be the *main* thing Christians are known for. Number two, Christianity is taking a massive PR hit for its perceived obsession with abortion, but doing almost nothing to actually combat abortion. Number three, in an effort to dispel the notion that all we care about is abortion, the church is becoming even *less* inclined to care for abortion-vulnerable children. We have a church that doesn't care much about abortion, a world that thinks *all* the church cares about is abortion, and Christians that are starting to believe it—almost apologizing for a fervor we simply don't have.

As much as I love *Good News About Injustice,* the Gary Haugen book I quoted at the outset of this chapter, I still find it odd that it bears no mention of abortion. Contemporary forms of injustice are chronicled in great detail, but aborted children are not included in any of the victim lists. Why is that? Why would a book expressly written to encourage the church to "extend the love of Jesus [to the] men, women, and children who are victimized by the abuse of power" entirely omit abortion?[12] A quick search introduced me to a 2009 article from *The New Yorker* that offered some insights. In that article, Haugen says:

> Evangelicals come from a tradition that says, "Don't be involved in politics. Try to go to Heaven." But then we entered a phase where the religious right said, "It's our duty as Christians to be involved in politics, and here's what Christians should be politically involved in fighting: abortion, gay rights, Communism." Now, today's Christians are saying, "Whoa, who says?" and "Surely there is more."[13]

In light of these remarks, I'd say the book's omission of abortion was a calculated one—owing to some combination of the following convictions: a) abortion is already being combated by the evangelical church b) abortion is not as serious a problem as child slavery, forced prostitution, prisoner torture, etc. c) abortion is too divisive an issue to make bridge-building possible. As the active pursuit of social justice gains traction in the evangelical church, there is a noticeable backlash underway—a backlash *against* taking a stand on abortion.

---

12 Haugen, Gary. *Good News About Injustice, Updated 10th Anniversary Edition: A Witness of Courage in a Hurting World.* (Downer's Grove: IVP Books, 2009) 26.

13 Power, Samantha. "The Enforcer." *The New Yorker*, 19 Jan. 2009. <hhttp://www.newyorker.com/reporting/2009/01/19/090119fa_fact_power#ixzz12k0cBj3m>.

Recently, I was at a large national conference on orphan care and adoption. One of the general session speakers made a tremendously compelling case for churches to realign their ministries in accordance with James 1:27. He said one of the most probing and revealing questions we can ask pastors is simply this, "How many orphans is your church caring for?" He went to Isaiah 58 to argue that the service God is looking for is not empty religiosity, but rather "to loose the bonds of wickedness… to let the oppressed go free… to share your bread with the hungry… [to] bring the homeless poor into your house, and [to clothe] the naked." (58:6,7) He said the Great Commission has become the Great Omission, and noted that, if every church in America adopted one child, foster care would be completely eradicated. Amen and amen. But then he said something that made me wince. Referring to the church, he said, "We'll picket abortion clinics and vote pro-life, but we don't care about kids after they're born."

There are a number of things that trouble me about this statement. I'll start with the relatively minor ones. First, the majority of people who stand outside abortion clinics are not "picketing." They are praying or counseling. Picketing is a negative term. It's the world's term used to belittle and demean those who feel strongly enough about the violent death of unborn children to actually interrupt their busy schedule, invite the scorn of their community, and publicly stand against it. Second, call it what you want, the majority of Christians have never set foot outside an abortion clinic, except perhaps to get *inside* the abortion clinic. When pastors like this one, with a tremendous heart for orphan care, make subtly derisive remarks about the relatively small percentage of Christians who actually *are* combating abortion, they're simply reinforcing the misconceptions of the world. Those are my minor points of contention. The main problem lies in the second half of the pastor's accusation. While I agree with his assessment that the evangelical church as a whole is not adequately caring for orphans, and I agree with his declaration that Christians should be known more for what we're for than what we're against, it is simply untrue to claim that those who are passionate about rescuing children from abortion don't care about these children once they're born. My experience has been exactly the opposite. Long before adoption became fashionable both inside and outside the church, those in the abortion battle were already adopting children in droves. For many years, it seemed the only people in the evangelical church who cared about adoption were the ones who cared about abortion.

If you start with the abortion problem, there is a natural gravitation towards adoption. You embrace adoption because it is a solution to abortion. I do not say *the* solution, for it is not a lack of adoptive parents that drives the abortion epidemic, but adoption is a glorious response to the existence of "unwanted" children. However, if you start with adoption as a response to the orphan crisis, you may not naturally move towards the active opposition of abortion. In fact, the world sees abortion as a solution to the orphan crisis, and it's possible that the church believes the same—though most would never admit it. There is a subtle perception in some modern, evangelical churches that adoption is loving and Christ-like, but opposition to abortion is hateful and Pharisaic.

More and more churches see widow and orphan care as central to the gospel of Christ, while claiming that abortion is "too political" to be involved with. I think what they mean is that abortion is too politically *unpopular* to be involved with. After all, there are plenty of political components to widow and orphan care. All social justice issues have political components. It is intellectually dishonest to argue that abortion is too political of an issue for Christians to get involved with, when all these other issues are *not* too political to get involved with. If standing against abortion were not such a socially unpopular position to take, I've no doubt the "too political" arguments would all but go away. Though the immediate context of James 2 is fairly narrow, the underlying theme is remarkably applicable. The sin of partiality is a horrible thing:

> My brothers, show no partiality as you hold the faith in our Lord Jesus Christ, the Lord of glory. For if a man wearing a gold ring and fine clothing comes into your assembly, and a poor man in shabby clothing also comes in, and if you pay attention to the one who wears the fine clothing and say, "You sit here in a good place," while you say to the poor man, "You stand over there," or, "Sit down at my feet," have you not then made distinctions

> among yourselves and become judges with
> evil thoughts?

James urges that we look past external appearances and not judge as the world does. As downtrodden and oppressed as widows and orphans are, abortion-vulnerable children are even worse off. They are smaller and weaker. They are more defenseless and in more immediate danger. They are helpless in every sense of the word. They cannot speak for themselves, and they have few advocates who will. John M. Perkins states that "in situations of inequality or oppression, the oppressed group *must* take a stand somewhere, sometime."[14] This is precisely what abortion-vulnerable children *cannot* do. Metaphorically, abortion-vulnerable children are the poor men in shabby clothing—being relegated to the back of the church. I say that not to belittle the very real needs of the multiple millions of orphaned children living in extreme poverty, but in simple recognition of the fact that they have a growing legion of advocates both inside and outside the church. Orphan care has never been so popular. I recently heard Matt Carter, the lead pastor at The Austin Stone Community Church, say he's "weary of Hollywood being a louder voice for the orphan than the church."[15] Giving credit where credit is due, we can thank God that so many in the entertainment industry and so many in corporate America have started intervening for the needs of orphaned children.

---

14 Perkins, John. *Let Justice Roll Down*. (Ventura: Regal, 1976) 115.
15 Carter, Matt, "The Church as the Champion of Social Justice" (Together for Adoption National Conference, October 2, 2010).

But what about abortion? In this arena, the philanthropy of Hollywood and Wall Street is almost exclusively directed *against* the orphan. As George Grant notes, Planned Parenthood, "the oldest, largest, and best-organized provider of abortion and birth-control services in the world, ... may well be the largest and most profitable nonprofit organization in history."[16] And two-thirds of their income comes from government grants and large corporate donations. Hollywood may love the orphan, but it also loves Planned Parenthood. We should ask then whether the church is taking our social justice cues from the Bible, from the world, or from somewhere in between.

In preparing for a talk I was to give to a group of Christian high school students, I did some research into the activism of today's top-selling Christian musicians. I checked iTunes for a list of the 10 most popular Christian artists and then visited their websites to see what kind of social justice causes they publicly support. Four of the artists didn't link to any third-party ministries. The rest linked to Imagine a Cure (juvenile diabetes), Compassion International (child advocacy), One Million Can (clean water, sex slavery, child soldiery, etc.), World Vision (international aid), TOMS Shoes (shoes for children), and Love + Hope + Help + Haiti (small business loans for women in Haiti). Not a single website made mention of the abortion issue, nor have I ever heard of a major label Christian artist that has made exposing

---

16 Grant, George. Foreword. *Abortion: A Rational Look at An Emotional Issue (20th Anniversary Edition)*. By R.C. Sproul. (Orlando: Reformation Trust, 1990, 2010) Xiii.

the injustice of abortion a ministry priority. I suspect the social cost of speaking out may simply be too high—much as it was 50 years ago. John Perkins writes:

> I had lived in the South. I had drunk at separate drinking fountains. I had ridden in the back of buses. And never in the South had I heard one white Christian speak out against the way whites treated blacks as second-class citizens.[17]

As it stands today, the evangelical church's renewed awakening to the physical needs of the marginalized and oppressed has largely been limited to the same social justice causes now being embraced by the world. This is dangerous. Galatians 1:10 comes to mind: "For am I now seeking the approval of man, or of God?..." In Luke 6:32-34, Jesus asks,

> If you love those who love you, what benefit is that to you? For even sinners love those who love them. And if you do good to those who do good to you, what benefit is that to you? For even sinners do the same. And if you lend to those from whom you expect to receive, what credit is that to you? Even sinners lend to sinners, to get back the same amount.

---

17 Perkins, John. *Let Justice Roll Down.* (Ventura: Regal, 1976) 56.

Christ commends the kind of love that serves people who have no capacity to serve us back. This is the kind of love that separates those who follow Christ from those who follow themselves.

It is a mercy that so much of the social activism God calls us to do makes Christianity more sympathetic and commendable to the unbelieving world. It is wonderful that we can enjoy the fruits of feeding the poor in the form of praise from the world and thanks from the victim. But are those the things that should be driving us? What if the world doesn't give us kudos? What if the victims have no capacity to thank us or recognize our efforts? Will we still act on their behalf? Isn't there a sort of beauty in moving forward on things close to God's heart for which there is no worldly reward? And isn't there a danger in only embracing causes that earn us the applause of the world—just as there is a danger in *never* embracing causes that earn the applause of the world?

I like how Tim Keller said it at the Desiring God National Conference some years back. In his words the world should be able to look at the church in any given community and say, "I don't like their approach to abortion, I don't like their approach to homosexuality, [but] if they left our city, we'd have to raise taxes [because] they're pressing so much of their heart and so much of their value into this city."[18] The unpopularity of standing against abortion should not deter the church from caring for abortion-vulnerable children

---

18 Keller, Tim. "The Supremacy of Christ and the Gospel in a Postmodern World" Desiring God National Conference. 30 Sep. 2006. <http://www.desiringgod.org/resource-library/conference-messages/the-supremacy-of-christ-and-the-gospel-in-a-postmodern-world>.

any more than the popularity of standing for the poor and oppressed should deter the church from caring for orphaned children.

I am not arguing that we become what the world *accuses* us of being: obsessed with abortion and indifferent to the myriad of other human injustices. Rather, I am arguing that we become what we *should* be: a church that loves people and combats injustice wherever it is found, even, and especially, when it is an injustice being ignored or celebrated by the world. For the church to simply jettison the abortion issue in an attempt to combat the notion that all we care about is abortion is a mistake—a huge mistake. So long as worldly wisdom can account for everything the church does, something is terribly wrong. It is when the watching world looks at our lives and our activism and can't account for it that the wheels start turning. The central premise of Tullian Tchividjian's book, *Unfashionable*, is that "Christians make a difference in this world by being different from this world."[19] For my part, I would simply qualify that there is a degree of "sameness" that is good and healthy. In some ways, those falling off the saddle on the personal piety side have made an idol of being detached from the world. We don't want our lives to look *so* foreign that we lose all connection. There is a place for common ground; there is a place for cultural overlap. In one sense we do want the world to see the church as being filled with people just like them—broken, hurting, sinful people in need of a savior. In another sense, we want

---

19 Tchividjian, Tullian. *Unfashionable* (Colorado Springs: Multnomah Books, 2009) 9.

the world to look at the church and scratch their heads. *Why would they embrace suffering and scorn? Why do they care so much about embryos and fetuses? Why do they give their money away?*

At the heart of the battle for biblical balance is the battle between being like the world and being different from the world. We want to bridge gaps; we want to demonstrate that Jesus loves people in physically tangible ways. We want to show that the message of Christ is good for the city and good for the soul. But when biblical justice and compassion is out of step with society's moral compass—as it is with abortion, when our activism becomes a barrier instead of a bridge—it is then that our true allegiance must be shown. Are we living for God or living for man? The personal piety side argues that abortion isn't mentioned in the Bible, it's not evangelism, it's a distraction from the central call of the church. The social justice side argues that abortion is divisive, unloving, and less important than other issues. One side doesn't touch abortion because it's too political; one side doesn't touch abortion because it's too unpopular. And both sides are wrong.

Conclusion

LOVE CHRIST (A LOT)

ABOUT TWO-THIRDS OF THE WAY THROUGH Harriet Beecher Stowe's classic, *Uncle Tom's Cabin*, the novel's child heroine is asked what it means to be a Christian. Her response to that question is the best I've ever heard. Being a Christian, Eva tells her father, means "Loving Christ most of all."[1] For those of us conditioned to see Christianity more as something to believe and less as a Savior to love, may this profoundly simple definition be an indictment for change. How many of the people who call themselves Christians truly love Jesus most of all? Do you? Do I?

The brilliance of Eva's assertion is twofold. First, it recognizes one of life's foundational truisms. No matter what we say, each of us makes an idol out of the person or thing we love the most. So unless Christ sits on the throne of my affections, I am an idolater. Second, Eva's definition combats the two most common distortions of Christianity. The first sees Christianity as a list of do's and don'ts; the second sees it as a license to live however you want. But if you understand

---

1   Stowe, Harriet Beecher. *Uncle Tom's Cabin*. Public Domain Books. Kindle Edition. 331.

Christianity to mean loving Jesus over and above everything else, it keeps you from either pitfall. To those in the first group it says, "OK, you go to church, you live a 'moral' life, but those things don't count for anything unless you LOVE Jesus!" To those in the second group it says, "You've signed a card and prayed a prayer, but that is nothing without LOVE for Jesus!"

I don't want anyone to get to the end of this book and think that being a Christian means doing things for God (like combating abortion) to earn his favor. But neither do I want you to get to the end of your life thinking that confession and belief are abstract one-time things. In what may be the most frightening passage in Scripture, Jesus says that on the day of judgment, many "Christians" will confidently cry out to him only to be turned away at the gate. Why? Because they didn't do the will of the Father. Stunned, they will ask, "Lord, Lord, did we not prophesy in your name, and cast out demons in your name, and do many mighty works in name?" Jesus will answer them, "I never knew you; depart from me, you workers of lawlessness." These men and women prophesied in Jesus' name, cast out demon's in Jesus' name, performed mighty works in Jesus' name, but Jesus turns them away and calls them "workers of lawlessness." Externally, their lives were marked by extraordinary acts of devotion. Internally, they didn't love Jesus. For anyone involved in ministry, these words should make us tremble. It is so easy to replace devotion to Christ with devotion to cause—while pursuing "success" according to the same self-exalting metrics as the world. Devotion to church, pastor, worship band, or youth group can be maintained in the flesh. Devotion to Christ is only possible through the power of the Holy Spirit.

On the other side of the spectrum, there is equal danger in thinking that love for Christ can be manifested apart from obedience to his commandments. You can externally obey the commandments without loving Jesus, but you can't love Jesus without obeying. Consider what Jesus says in John 14: "If you love me, you will keep my commandments... Whoever has my commandments and keeps them, he it is who loves me... If anyone loves me, he will keep my word... Whoever does not love me does not keep my words." Loving Jesus means far more than just having a positive impression of him or thinking him a cool guy. Jesus says, "Whoever loves father or mother more than me is not worthy of me, and whoever loves son or daughter more than me is not worthy of me. And whoever does not take his cross and follow me is not worthy of me."[2] Or how about this?

> So Jesus said to them, "Truly, truly, I say to you, unless you eat the flesh of the Son of Man and drink his blood, you have no life in you. Whoever feeds on my flesh and drinks my blood has eternal life, and I will raise him up on the last day. For my flesh is true food, and my blood is true drink. Whoever feeds on my flesh and drinks my blood abides in me, and I in him. As the living Father sent me, and I live because of the Father, so whoever

---

2   Matthew 10:37-38

feeds on me, he also will live because of me. This is the bread that came down from heaven, not like the bread the fathers ate, and died. Whoever feeds on this bread will live forever."

As C.S. Lewis (and later Bono) noted, Jesus is a liar, a lunatic, or the King of Kings. He leaves room for no other option. Love him or hate him, but don't fall prey to the fuzzy, "Jesus is my homeboy" silliness. Either you orient your entire life around him or you reject him as a heretic and blasphemer. My assumption is that a lot people reading this have great fervor for life or great fervor for ministry, but very little fervor for Jesus. You don't hate him; you just sort of forget about him in the busyness of life. Revelation 3:15-16 comes to mind: "I know your works: you are neither cold nor hot. Would that you were either cold or hot! So, because you are lukewarm, and neither hot nor cold, I will spit you out of my mouth." There is honor in being loved. There is even honor in being hated. There is no honor in being ignored.

As I've thought about my own failure to treasure Christ as he deserves, this is where I've landed. When we think much of ourselves, we think little of Christ. It is only when we recognize our intrinsic selfishness and depravity that Christ becomes lovely and precious—our All in All. Part of my preparation for chapter five included reading through Matthew, Mark, Luke, and John to write down every commandment Jesus issued. There are numerous commandments related to religious devotion (prayer, fasting, meditation, etc.), loving others, combating sin, and being wise, but hardly any related to evangelism. In fact, the commandments *against* evangelism are far more prevalent:

> And Jesus stretched out his hand and touched him… And immediately his leprosy was cleansed. And Jesus said to him, "See that you say nothing to anyone…"[3]

> And their eyes were opened. And Jesus sternly warned them, "See that no one knows about it."[4]

> Many followed him, and he healed them all and ordered them not to make him known.[5]

> Then he strictly charged the disciples to tell no one that he was the Christ.[6]

> And whenever the unclean spirits saw him, they fell down before him and cried out, "You are the Son of God." And he strictly ordered them not to make him known.[7]

Why did Jesus so often forbid people to publicly make him known? Luke gives us the best answer. Following Peter's declaration that Jesus is "The Christ of God," Jesus "strictly

3   Matthew 8:3-4
4   Matthew 9:30
5   Matthew 12:15-6
6   Matthew 16:20
7   Mark 3:11-12

charged and commanded [the disciples] to tell this to no one, saying, 'The Son of Man must suffer many things and be rejected by the elders and chief priests and scribes, and be killed, and on the third day be raised.'"[8] Jesus didn't come to be crowned; he came to be killed. The time for full proclamation had not yet arrived. But there is something else worth noting. Many of the people Jesus healed couldn't help but proclaim what he did for them—despite his prohibitions. Jesus went to great lengths to keep a lid on his popularity, but word still spread like wildfire. He drew crowds wherever he went. People who are excited about something need no prodding to talk about it. They can't help themselves. When you've been broken your whole life and then you're fixed, oh joy!—that is something to shout from the rooftops.

If proclaiming Christ is a duty, it's because we've forgotten how broken we are—or perhaps we've never been healed at all. Like the Pharisees, we think ourselves healthy; we think ourselves wise; we think ourselves moral. But if proclaiming Christ is a delight—the natural outpouring of a satisfied soul—it is because we rightly see ourselves as the publican: "God, be merciful to me, a sinner!"[9] My goal each day is to be happy enough in Jesus that I want to tell people about it. To that end, this is my best effort to explain the good news:

> Everyone on the planet lives in the shadow
> of the unknown, which means we're all living

---

8 Luke 9:21-22
9 Luke 18:13

by faith. For my part, I believe the Bible, not because it answers all my questions or eliminates all my doubts, but because it has the only reasonable explanation for the realities I see in and around me. It provides a plausible account of how this massive, intricately complex universe came to be and explains why there is a constant tension playing out in my head.

The Bible tells a history that is too bizarre to be fabricated about a Savior God who is too unconventional to spring from the minds of men. There is no earthly reason why the brief life of a poor, uneducated Jewish carpenter should have more global influence than any other life in history. And the only conceivable rationale for why a band of heretofore cowardly men would literally sacrifice their lives to proclaim salvation through Jesus Christ is because they witnessed His resurrection from the dead and were changed forever. The only way their influence could have enough traction to span the globe, and ultimately rewrite human history, is for it to be driven by divine means.

The Bible is the story of the eternal God who spoke the world into existence, and then witnessed the prize of His creation, a perfect man and perfect woman, rebel against his generous authority, placing all of the created order under a curse. The fallout for us is that, because of the sin of Adam, the first representative of the human race, we are all born condemned—with a natural antagonism towards God's authority in our lives. Each of us is like one who comes out of a coma in the middle of a war, gun in hand, firing blindly at an unknown enemy and having no idea why. We weren't around when the sides were chosen, and we compromise ourselves long before we even know we're at war. And the penalty for rebelling against our perfect, holy, Creator God? Eternal torment. But before we cry out, "Unfair!!" consider this: God in his mercy made a pathway for restoration. Just as sin entered the world through one man and death through sin, so the free gift—forgiveness of sins!—is made possible through one man, Jesus Christ. God, the Son, entered his creation in the form of a man, born to a virgin, tempted in every way and yet without sin. He submitted himself to be crucified according to the preordained will of the Father for claiming to be exactly who he was—God in human flesh. But Jesus rose from the dead three days later, ministered on earth in his resurrected body, and physically ascending into the clouds—promising to return again in the same way.

What must we do to have Jesus' righteousness applied to our account? Repent and believe. That is, we must stop rebelling against the ordinances of God, confess our spiritual helplessness, and cling to the life and death of Jesus Christ. We must believe he is God and that he rewards those who seek him![10] To the broken, humble and hurting, Jesus says, "Come to me...my yoke is easy and my burden is light."[11] To

---

10 Hebrews 11:6
11 Matthew 11:28,30

those unwilling to admit their blindness, he says "[Because] you say, 'We see,' your guilt remains."[12]

I said at the beginning of this book that there is a parallel between the sin of abortion and the universal sinfulness of man. So there is. Every sin is an act of rebellion against the authority of God—a declaration that we know better, that we will be our own god. The tragic irony is that God's commands are not punishments, they are protections. We violate them to our own destruction—complaining about suffering and injustice in the world, forgetting that they only exist because of *our* rebellion. Why do we blame God for the damage caused by our rejection of his holy commands? In light of what we've done, it's a miracle the world isn't in worse shape than it is. And though God has the power to restore everything to its former glory, he has something even bigger in view.[13]

In the context of abortion, our refusal to yield to God's authority manifests itself on many levels. The fact that 84% of all U.S. abortions are performed on unmarried women testifies of our failure to yield to the authority of God in our sex lives. The fact that 75% of all U.S. abortions are performed on women who say they can't afford a baby testifies of our failure to trust God and be anxious for nothing. The fact that 75% of aborting women also say a child would interfere with their personal or professional lives testifies of our failure to understand that it is more blessed to give than to receive. The fact that 67% of all U.S. abortions are performed on women who claim the name of Christ testifies of our failure to make

---

12 John 9:41
13 I Corinthians 2:9, Revelation 2:10

disciples, teaching all that Christ has commanded. The fact that 3% of all U.S. abortions are performed on children with potential fetal abnormalities testifies of our failure to realize that those born with disabilities have been made that way so "the works of God might be displayed."[14] Abortion is what happens when human beings try to usurp the authority of God. We "fix" problems by making them infinitely worse. Or as James 4:2 says, *we desire and do not have so we murder. We covet and cannot obtain, so we fight and quarrel.* The perennial discontent of the human heart is strong evidence that we are running from the only thing that can ever satisfy us:[15] *"The sorrows of those who run after another god shall multiply..."*[16] Thankfully, it is also sorrow that leads to repentance.[17] So whether you've had a dozen abortions or helped shut down a dozen abortion clinics, your standing before God is the same: "All have sinned and fall short of the glory of God."[18] This is why the path to redemption is the same for the abortionist as it is for the abolitionist—and for the time being, it stands open to all. It is not love for Christ that makes us worthy of redemption. It is the *blood* of Christ that makes us worthy—and the only fit response is to love Christ most of all.

---

14 John 9:3
15 Psalm 16:11
16 Psalm 16:4
17 2 Corinthians 7:10
18 Romans 3:23

THE UNIQUE AND PROPHETIC PLACE OF ABORT73.COM

RESOLVING TO DO SOMETHING about abortion is the easy part. Figuring out what to do is decidedly harder. How do you intervene for a victim-class that can't be seen? How do you save invisible children from being legally killed? The solution to some problems is obvious. The solution to the abortion problem is not—which is why I want to further introduce you to Abort73.com. In 2002, I read a book by John Piper called, *Brothers, We Are Not Professionals*. He devotes an entire chapter to the topic of abortion and concludes it with this charge:

> … support alternatives to abortion with your money and time and prayers. Find out about concrete opportunities that are available in our region for all kinds of involvement. *Even better, create new pro-life ministries. Let's be a church of dreamers and entrepreneurs for justice* (emphasis added).[1]

---

1   Piper, John. *Brothers, We Are Not Professionals*. (Nashville: Broadman & Holman Publishers, 2002) 226-27.

In the shadow of those last two sentences, Abort73.com was born. I don't know why John Piper called the creation of new pro-life ministries "even better" than involvement with existing ones, but I have an idea. When he made this plea, abortion had already been legal in the United States for 29 years. And for 29 years, significant time and resources were spent combating abortion with little to show for it. Mandatory waiting periods and parental consent requirements were enacted in *some* states, but abortion remained legal in *every* state—through all nine months of pregnancy. And though the number of U.S. abortions had been in decline since its peak in 1990, the progress was painstakingly slow. In the 10-years prior to Piper's remarks, the annual decrease was only about 1% per year. Some will argue that if even one life was saved, then it was all worth it. But what if that energy could have been better spent to save even more lives? Doesn't the parable of the talents[2] commend us to seek a maximum return on our ministry investment?

Over the years, the lion's share of pro-life labor and resources has been invested on two fronts: political engagement and crisis-pregnancy care. Abort73 is part of a growing field of ministries that is pushing a third front: education. For too long, we've put the cart before the horse. Yes, we must change the law, but minds must be changed first. So long as the populace is indifferent to abortion, so long as they see it as a minor problem or a necessary evil, we won't have anywhere near the national resolve necessary to enact sweeping change. Likewise, while assisting women in crisis

2   Matthew 25:14-30

pregnancies must always be a part of pro-life engagement, it should never be the only part. Crisis pregnancy care is reactive. It meets individual needs, but it doesn't reform the system. And until more women (and men) better understand what abortion is and does, they'll continue to pass by the pregnancy care centers, on their way to Planned Parenthood. Unless we do a better job at reaching people *before* they're in crisis, we'll continue to miss them when they're in crisis.

My own pro-life engagement began in 1999 when I joined The Center for Bio-Ethical Reform (CBR) as part of the Genocide Awareness Project. It didn't take long to realize that people on both sides of the abortion debate tend to be more familiar with the slogans than they are with the facts. Abortion may be one of the most common surgical procedures in the world, but an accurate abortion education is hard to come by. It's not provided by most schools or churches; it's not provided by most media outlets, and it's certainly not provided by the abortion clinics themselves. Abortion thrives by lingering in the shadows.

The Genocide Awareness Project is a gigantic photo-mural exhibit that sets up in the middle of state universities and compares abortion to historically-recognized forms of genocide. The strength of the project is that it brings an extremely compelling abortion education directly to college students, bypassing the traditional, scholastic gatekeepers. The weakness of the project is that it can't be in all places at once. It is staff and equipment-intensive, which makes it virtually impossible to visit enough schools each year to gain critical mass. And it can't reach high school or middle school students at all. Here enters Abort73.

From the very outset, Abort73 has existed for two reasons: to educate and activate. As a stand-alone resource, Abort73.com took much of what makes the Genocide Awareness Project so compelling and infinitely expanded its audience. We operate on the principle that the more someone knows about abortion, the less likely they are to have one, recommend one, or support one as a matter of public policy. Abort73.com can give you a basic overview of abortion in two minutes, or you can spend two days on the site without exhausting its content. But no matter how compelling the case against abortion, it will never change any minds until it finds an audience—which is why the second half of Abort73's mandate is no less crucial than the first.

Traditionally, for a message to make any cultural headway, it must have the backing of significant cash reserves or a sympathetic press corps. The case against abortion has neither. Thankfully, these traditional barriers are rapidly collapsing—done in by the World Wide Web. Never before has there been such a remarkable outlet for putting marginalized viewpoints in front of the masses. But while websites have theoretical access to an entire world of people, they must compete with millions of other sites for attention. In the case of abortion, gaining an audience can be even harder since there is so much baggage tied to this issue. How many people are naturally inclined to subject themselves to an ethical analysis of such a controversial issue? Since Abort73 lacks the financial backing or political connections to embark on a more traditional advertising blitz, and since we've tied ourselves to a cause with all sorts of negative connotations, we've embraced a decidedly untraditional strategy for making the case against abortion.

It starts with our name, which is an intentionally vague URL. Though conventional wisdom recommends a more descriptive moniker, that wasn't our goal. Why? Because we're fighting against misconceptions and complacency. Many people have stereotyped opposition to abortion as mere religious fanaticism. Others have no desire to involve themselves in such a divisive issue. For all of these people, a more descriptive name would likely keep us from even getting a hearing. To help avoid that, we chose a URL that communicates very little, and we've printed that URL on tens of thousands of T-shirts. Each one exists to prompt the question, "What is Abort73.com?"—a question that naturally leads people to the website.

So what does the name Abort73 actually mean? The connection becomes clear after watching our intro video, *January 1973*, which plays on the Abort73 homepage. We took the word "abortion" and shortened it to "abort." Next, we took the year in which the U.S. Supreme Court struck down all state prohibitions against abortion, 1973, and shortened it to "73." When put together, you can look at the name in two ways. Either it is an abbreviation of Abortion 1973, or it is a resource to help "abort" (terminate) the fallout of that 1973 verdict. Both work, and both were in view when the name was chosen.

While Abort73 offers a broad, abortion education to people of all ages, we are the most anxious to reach students and young adults. Young people tend to be more open-minded, more willing to change their mind, and less-likely to have a personal stake in justifying abortion. Plus, more than half of all abortions are performed on women younger than 25. Changing the way our culture thinks about abortion begins with changing the way our students think about abortion. And that brings us back to the Abort73 T-shirts, which are the backbone of our marketing campaign.

T-shirts are great for slogans, but slogans don't prove anything. And unless we prove that abortion is immoral and unjust, nothing will ever change. That's why Abort73 has adopted an equally unconventional approach for our T-shirts. Instead of expecting a shirt to do the educating (something it's not much good at), Abort73 shirts point people to a free, almost universally-accessible resource where they actually *can* be educated. Why? Because the Abort73 website does things that T-shirts can't. It takes people past the mere expression of opinion, straight to the evidence which compels that opinion. Websites have the capacity to educate in ways that not even books or films can duplicate—let alone a T-shirt!

So why do we bother with T-shirts at all? Because T-shirts do things that websites can't! They walk the streets. They get on busses. They sit in classrooms. T-shirts have a built in audience and don't require the consent of those who view them. The relationship between the Abort73 shirts and the Abort73 website is an extremely strategic one. The T-shirts, without the website, would be useless, and the website, without the T-shirts, would be largely ignored. They need each other. And it doesn't end with the T-shirts. We've got Abort73 pens, stickers, bracelets, buttons, promo cards, web graphics, and flyers that all function the same way. Each one is a pointer to Abort73.com.

If you visit the *Bringing an End to Abortion* section of the website, you'll find a list of the "Top-Ten Ways to Help," and they're certainly not all tied to buying Abort73 products. In fact, we have a separate top-ten list that is entirely devoted to promoting Abort73 within your social network, and everything on the list is entirely free. We have another top-ten list for bands and musicians and two pages of ideas for campus clubs and student ministry groups. Abort73 is what it is by the grace of God *through* the active promotion of groups and individuals around the world. The reason we offer so many simple entry points for involvement isn't because we want people to be able to say they're doing something about abortion. It's because we can't reach enough campuses or communities without them. Our success is absolutely dependent upon the efforts of others on our behalf. So, if you happen to be looking for a way to engage on the abortion front, we happen to be looking for people willing to introduce Abort73 to their campus or community! Think of it this way. Abort73 connects you to the truth about abortion, and you connect the world to Abort73.

WHY IT IS WRONG TO KILL AN ABORTIONIST

On May 31, 2009, George Tiller, the most notorious abortionist in the country was murdered in the lobby of Reformation Lutheran Church in Wichita, KS— where he was serving as an usher. A few days later, I posted the following blog, to help articulate why it is immoral and unjust to combat abortion through violence.

FOR THE LAST TWO DAYS, a steady stream of press releases has poured into my inbox—all of them from pro-life organizations rightly condemning the murder of late-term abortionist, Dr. George Tiller. I would like to join their chorus. From our inception, Abort73 has publicly denounced all such actions. They are cowardly, immoral and ultimately, damaging to the cause. Our official position statement reads: "Abort73 does not support or condone violence against abortion providers nor associate with groups that do."

Condemning the murder of Dr. Tiller is the easy part. Explaining why his death is condemnable is a bit harder—which may be why so few of the press releases I've read even made the effort. The tension is this. George Tiller was an abortionist. He made his living killing the most helpless members of the human community. *The Washington Times* estimates that over the course of his life, Dr. Tiller performed 60,000 abortions,[1] often on fetuses old enough to survive outside the womb. It is hard to imagine a more sinister vocation (how many other men can you think of who have personally killed upwards of 60,000 human beings?)!

Had Dr. Tiller's life continued, he may well have performed thousands of abortions more. We can only assume that the man who killed Dr. Tiller rationalized his actions this way: *If the law won't intervene, I will.* You see the moral tension. The fact that our government currently protects an abortionist's "right" to kill human beings in the womb creates HUGE ethical and philosophical problems. So how do we demonstrate the fallacy of taking the law into your own hands, when the law fails to protect the lives of helpless, unborn children? Most of the statements of condemnation I've seen read something like this:

> It is never consistent with the pro-life ethic
> to take the life of another human being made
> in the image of God.

---

1   "Pro-lifers vow to oppose Sebelius." *The Washington Times*. 28 Feb. 2009.
     <http://www.washingtontimes.com/news/2009/feb/28/pro-life-groups-
     vow-to-fight-sebelius-pick/>.

> A true, pro-life person respects human life as
> a gift from God, and leaves all life and death
> decisions to God Himself.

The problem I have with these statements is that they're too simplistic. They don't adequately deal with the philosophical underpinnings that drive this sort of vigilante justice. Consider this scenario. What would have happened if the man who killed Dr. Tiller didn't flee from the church after the murder? What if he had stayed there and continued to shoot other church members? What if he had set his sights on the nursery? If any of us were faced with the question of either allowing a gunman to shoot at helpless children or using deadly force to stop him, would we still say that, "it is never consistent with the pro-life ethic to take the life of another human being"? If not, then is that really a sufficient rationale for condemning the murder of Dr. Tiller? If it is legitimate in one instance to use deadly force to keep someone from killing helpless children, we must be able to explain why it is NOT legitimate in this instance. Of all the statements I've read this week, I think the NRLC's comes the closest. They say:

> The pro-life movement works to protect the
> right to life and increase respect for human
> life. The *unlawful* use of violence is directly
> contrary to that goal (emphasis added).[2]

---

2   "National Right To Life Condemns The Killing Of Dr. George Tiller." Press
    Release. National Right to Life. 31 May 2009. <http://www.nrlc.org/press_
    releases_new/Release053109.html>.

The primary difference between killing children in the womb and killing children in the nursery is that the law allows for one, but not the other. Even for those of us who claim allegiance to a higher authority than the state, that is not an insignificant distinction. Romans 13:1 tells us that all governing authorities, good and bad, have been instituted by God. Whoever resists the authorities, resists what God has appointed. Though the Bible does provide some legitimate examples of civil disobedience, they are clearly a measure of last resort. More to the point, none of the biblical examples endorse violence or imply that violence is a legitimate means of resisting unjust laws.

Perhaps the clearest scriptural indictment against violently taking the law into your own hands comes from the Garden of Gethsemane.[3] Jesus the Christ, God incarnate, creator of the universe, has just been betrayed. To protect him from a death that can be called nothing less than the greatest injustice in human history (an injustice that far exceeds even the destruction of unborn children), Peter draws his sword in defense of innocent human life. He swings at the head of the high priest's servant and cuts off his ear. If there was ever a situation that necessitated violent, civil disobedience, surely this was it. But all Peter earns for his efforts is a rebuke from Christ:

> Put your sword back into its place. For all
> who take the sword will perish by the sword.
> Do you think that I cannot appeal to my

---

3   Matthew 26:47-54

> Father and he will at once send me more
> than twelve legions of angels? But how then
> should the Scriptures be fulfilled, that it must
> be so?[4]

God the Father could have rescued Christ from the cross, just as he could have rescued all the children that have lost their lives to abortion. For some reason, that's not his plan. And not only that, he tells Peter to put the sword away. Looking back, we can see God's design in allowing his own Son to suffer and die. Someday we'll look back and see God's design in allowing so many unborn children to die. Abortion, as I've said before, is both deserving of God's wrath and an outpouring of God's wrath. God's hands are not tied. He doesn't need individual citizens to kill people in the name of justice. Every life is at his disposal already.

Why was it was wrong to kill Dr. Tiller? Because Dr. Tiller was a law-abiding citizen. He did no more than the law allowed him to do. You don't kill a man for doing something that the law (even an arguably unjust law) allows. You work at changing the law. Though killing children inside the womb and killing children outside the womb are moral equivalents for many of us, for many others they are not. There is no debate over the morality of killing human infants, but there is a huge debate over the morality of killing human fetuses. You don't bridge that moral gap by killing abortionists, you bridge it by demonstrating why abortion is morally akin to infanticide.

---

4   Matthew 26:52-54

There are times when the state must decide whether it is legitimate or not to employ deadly force in the service of peace, but citizens are not endowed with that same authority—at least not outside of those extremely rare circumstances where an assailant is breaking the law and threatening the lives of other people. Because punishing the guilty is the state's responsibility, the state is accountable to God for rightly executing his judgment. We are not. That doesn't mean we can take a pass when faced with suffering and injustice. It simply means that we must work within the many legitimate, God-given means for enacting change. God's people do have a responsibility to intervene on behalf of abortion-vulnerable children, but part of that responsibility is to intervene in ways that are both righteous and wise. Killing doctors is neither.

The main problem is not the individual men who perform abortions. The problem is the system that allows them to legally kill children. Abortionists can be replaced. In fact, Kim Gandy, president of the National Organization for Women (NOW) believes that "[the murder of George Tiller] will inspire another doctor to take up the torch, and another, and another."[5] She's probably right. There's something sympathetic, even heroic about dying for your cause. As a result of one shortsighted, cowardly, "one and done" act of violence, an otherwise shameful doctor suddenly becomes a martyr. His killer will spend the rest of his life in jail—useless to his family, useless to his friends, and useless to the cause he

5   Gandy, Kim. "NOW Identifies Murder of Dr. George Tiller As Domestic Terrorism, Calls for Action from Justice Department and Homeland Security." Press Release. National Organization for Women. 1 June 2009. <http://www.now.org/press/06-09/06-01.html>.

claims to support. The rest of us are left to pick up the pieces as we fight off all the accusations trying to link non-violent, pro-life activism with the barbarism of one man.

I will grant that the murder of George Tiller likely spared the lives of some children. It is reasonable to assume that in the months to come, children will be born, who would have been aborted had Dr. Tiller not lost his life. That, however, does not justify the act. It is a remarkable mercy of God that good things can result from wicked actions. Out of wedlock births are a prime example. The Bible is clear that sex outside of marriage is sin, and yet how many blessed children have been born out of such unions? In the United States, we have historically unprecedented opportunities to peacefully, lawfully remedy all manner of injustices. We must use them, because killing abortionists is not the way to end abortion.

Appendix C

WHO ARE THE LEAST OF THESE?

THROUGH THE YEARS, the "least of these" tag has been applied to a broad range of poor and oppressed people—a practice that may be a distortion of Matthew's immediate context. Notice what Jesus says in Matthew 25:40, in his address to those on his right:

> And the King will answer them, "Truly, I say to you, as you did it to one of the least of these *my brothers*, you did it to me" (emphasis added).

The designation, "brothers" or "brethren," generally refers to believers, which leads some commentators to conclude that when Jesus says the "least of these my brothers," he is not referring to social outcasts in general, but to mistreated, tribulation saints in particular. My own leaning is that "my brothers" in this context, refers more to the brotherhood of humanity than to the brotherhood of the church. I say that for two reasons. The first ties to Jesus' use of the word "brothers" in Matthew 5:22 and 23:8. In Matthew 23:8, Jesus is in the temple addressing a large and varied group of people. The account begins in Matthew 21:23 and goes all the way to the end of chapter 23. At various points in the conversation, he is questioned by chief priests, elders, Pharisees, Herodians and Sadducees. Matthew 23:1 tells us explicitly that Jesus' words in this chapter are directed "to the crowds and to his disciples." He opens by condemning the self-exaltation of the scribes and Pharisees and says in verse eight: "But you are not to be called rabbi, for you have one teacher and you are all brothers." Because so many in the crowd were hostile to his teaching, it is fairly safe to conclude that Jesus is not calling them brothers in a kingdom sense. And since there were almost certainly Gentiles in the crowd,[1] it is unlikely that Jesus is using "brothers" in a merely national sense either. The emphasis is on the unique supremacy of Christ (v11), and the generic equality of everyone else.

In Matthew 5:22, speaking to the crowds who gathered for the Sermon on the Mount, Jesus says, "But I say to you that everyone who is angry with his brother will be liable to judgment; whoever insults his brother will be liable to the council; and whoever says, 'You fool!' will be liable to the hell of fire." Though we can't say for certain how Jesus is defining the term "brother" here, it is reasonable to assume he's using it in the broadest sense possible. Would anyone read this passage and conclude that Jesus is only condemning hatred towards fellow believers or fellow Israelites? In the verses that

---

1   The greek word for temple, Hieros, in Matthew 23:21 and 24:1 denotes the area surrounding the temple, including the Court of Gentiles, in distinction from the temple building proper

follow (23-25), Jesus references a situation in which a brother is also an accuser—as if to say, *this man may not be your friend, but he is your brother*. The reason that hatred is such an absurd and inappropriate response is because it is directed against a *brother*. But if we take "brother" to only mean those of your same religion or ethnicity, the force of the argument largely vanishes.

Returning to the account of the sheep and the goats, the second reason I'm inclined to think "my brothers" spans the redemptive divide is because of the parallel statement we find in Matthew 25:45. Just as the sheep are ushered into the kingdom for their service to the least of these, the goats are sent into eternal fire for their negligence towards the least of these" If the "least of these" in this passage only refers to the redeemed, wouldn't it be odd for Jesus to condemn those *outside* the church for not caring for those *inside* the church? And here's where it gets even trickier. When Jesus refers to the least of these a second time, in his condemnation of those on his left, he does not qualify them as "my brothers." He simply states, "as you did not do it to one of the least of these, you did not do it to me." Do we then conclude that Jesus is referencing two separate groups that are both designated as the "least of these"—one among the sheep and one among the goats? Or is the same group being referred to in both instances, on slightly different terms? If the pronoun "these" refers to the "least" among the sheep in verse 40, does it refer to the "least" among the goats in verse 45, or is it still referencing the first group? If only we could see to which side Jesus was pointing when designating the "least of these"!

I close my case by conceding the possibility that I am wrong in my understanding of "brothers" in this passage. I'm well aware that the commentators I'm disagreeing with could run circles around me in theological debate. But even if Jesus' reference to the "least of these" does have a relatively narrow, eschatological focus, I don't think the application is materially changed. If Jesus is only commending service to the redeemed in this particular instance, he commends service to the masses in several other instances. Consider Matthew 5:43-47. Shortly after his words on anger, Jesus pushes the envelope even further with his command to love your enemies. In verses 43-44, he says, "You have heard that it was said, 'You shall love your neighbor and hate your enemy. But I say to you, Love your enemies and pray for those who persecute you.'" Then in verses 46-47, Jesus asks, "For if you love those how love you, what reward to you have? Do not even the tax collectors do the same? And if you greet only your brothers, what more are you doing than others? Do not even the Gentiles do the same?" Notice that Jesus seems to be using the words neighbor and brother interchangeably.

In one sense, verse 47 defines "brothers" more narrowly than I did in my reading of Matthew 25. When Jesus is critical of those who only love their brother, he implies the existence of non-brothers—a category of people that doesn't exist in the broader, brotherhood of humanity context. In another sense, this verse affirms exactly what I have been trying to demonstrate. Jesus says it is relatively easy to love your brothers. Everyone does that, including Gentiles and tax collectors. It is only God's people who love their enemies. Brotherhood, in this context seems to indicate those who have a natural affinity or connection to each other. When Jesus observes that everyone greets their brothers, it becomes obvious that here, too, "brothers" is not being used in a fellowship of believers sense. Unlike the Gentiles and tax collectors, who define "neighbor" and "brother" as narrowly as possible, Jesus calls us to expand these categories to include even our enemies. And if Jesus expects us to love our enemies, who are clearly not numbered among the redeemed, wouldn't he also expect us to love the "least of these," even when *they're* not numbered among the redeemed? If you only look for the "least of these" within the walls of the church—particularly in America, you may not find them at all. Many of the "least of these" simply aren't there. More times than not, it is tangible acts of love that get them to church in the first place. So even if "my brothers" does refer to the redeemed, isn't possible that the acts of service were performed *before* they were redeemed?

No matter where you land in your understanding of Matthew 25, there is no getting around the myriad of passages which indicate that Jesus *does* care how we treat the least of these in the world at large. I appreciate the desire to be contextually accurate and to not simply bend Scripture to say what we want it to say, but there is danger in pressing the narrow application too dogmatically (much like the lawyer in the story of the Good Samaritan). If it's a question of applying the "least of these" label too narrowly or applying it too broadly, can there be any debate as to which side we should error on?